IMAGES
of America

THE TORREY PINES GLIDERPORT

On the Cover: Spectators line the cliffs at the Torrey Pines Gliderport, watching the sailplanes soar effortlessly by in silent flight. San Diego's love affair with aviation first took hold with gliders and later blossomed at the Torrey Pines Gliderport, one of America's most unique soaring institutions. (Courtesy of the Soaring Society of America.)

IMAGES
of America

THE TORREY PINES GLIDERPORT

Gary B. Fogel

ARCADIA
PUBLISHING

ISBN 978-1-4671-3136-0

Published by Arcadia Publishing
Charleston, South Carolina

Printed in the United States of America

Library of Congress Control Number: 2013947819

For all general information, please contact Arcadia Publishing:
Telephone 843-853-2070
Fax 843-853-0044
E-mail sales@arcadiapublishing.com
For customer service and orders:
Toll-Free 1-888-313-2665

Visit us on the Internet at www.arcadiapublishing.com

To all glider pilots who share the tradition of soaring at Torrey Pines,
and to Joanne and Sabrina for their love and support.

Contents

Acknowledgments

The author would like to thank many individuals and organizations for their generosity and time in sharing their stories and photographs of soaring at Torrey Pines. In particular, Frank Allen III, Richard Benbough, Raul Blacksten, Ruth Bowlus, Woody Brown, Silvia Colton, Bob Fronius, Doug Fronius, Helen Dick, Craig Harwood, Joseph Lincoln, Bill Liscomb, Vincent Loop, Paul MacCready, Doug Perl, Alan Regna of the San Diego Air and Space Museum, John Robinson, Bertha Ryan, Judy Schulman, Ernie Shattuck, Bob Storck, George Uvegas, and June Wiberg.

Thanks also to those individuals and organizations who have sought to protect the Torrey Pines Gliderport as a unique recreational resource for the enjoyment of current and future generations of silent aviators, including Tom Crouch and Russell Lee of the National Air and Space Museum; Bill Gallagher, Simine Short, and the National Soaring Museum; Jeff Byard, Doug Fronius, and the members of the Vintage Sailplane Association; Harry Baldwin, Steve Kesckes, and members of the 1-26 Association; Brad Hall, Angelo Orona, Sal Peluso, Joe Holtzman, and members of the Torrey Pines Soaring Council; Bruce and Alana Coons and members of the Save Our Heritage Organization; Rolf Schulze, Byron Lowry, Ed Slater, Steve Pachura, Bud Robinson, and members of the Associated Glider Clubs of Southern California; Rich Hanson, Joyce Hager, Lawrence Tougas, and the Academy of Model Aeronautics; Patricia Schaelchlin, John Bolthouse, Donald Yeckel, and members of the La Jolla Historical Society; Vonn Marie May; and Milfred Wayne Donaldson.

Thank you to the countless pilots who have participated in more than 80 years of soaring at Torrey Pines and continue to inspire others, as Paul MacCready would say, to "do more with less," and to Alyssa Jones for her assistance in the production of this book. Most importantly, I would like to acknowledge the efforts of my mother and father, Eva and Larry Fogel, who instilled in me both the gift of soaring and the importance of perseverance at an early age.

INTRODUCTION

From John J. Montgomery's first glides in the 1880s, San Diegans have always held a particular fascination for silent flight. An idyllic combination of wind, climate, and geography led many to realize their own dreams of flight with gliders. In the 1920s and into the 1930s, aviators such as William Hawley Bowlus crafted ever more efficient designs, airplanes so sleek that they could soar above their point of takeoff in the proper conditions—without the need of a motor. American soaring endurance records quickly fell, raising national awareness of San Diego as a gliding capital. In 1930, Charles and Anne Lindbergh specifically came to San Diego to learn the art of soaring from Bowlus. A new generation of youngsters viewed gliding as an inexpensive way to take to the skies, to be just like Lucky Lindy. On a flight in February 1930, Charles Lindbergh used the lift above the cliffs at Torrey Pines to extend one of his soaring adventures. It was the first use of the lift at Torrey Pines by a glider pilot. Little did he realize at the time that his adventure heralded an entirely new resource for the sport, a future gliderport of international significance: the Torrey Pines Gliderport.

Following Lindbergh's success, enthusiastic high school students built their own gliders and flew them from the beach at Torrey Pines, using cars to tow them into the sky, soaring effortlessly on the lift provided by the cliffs, and returning to land on the beach. As with surfing or sailing, soaring was environmentally friendly, a clean scientific undertaking with the cliffs at Torrey Pines as a perfect outdoor testing facility. Technological advancements at Torrey Pines led directly to advances elsewhere, including the design of lighter-weight surfboards and high-speed catamarans—all under the shared spirit of working with nature rather than competing against nature. These youngsters epitomized the free spirit of California.

Glider pilots such as John Robinson, Woody Brown, Dick Essery, and Ray Parker spent hours aloft at Torrey Pines on the weekends, studying and refining their craft. As "Air Capital of the West," San Diego was already an aviation center. During the 1930s, each major local aviation company had its own glider club, with their aviators joining the Associated Glider Clubs of Southern California operating at Torrey Pines. The mayor of San Diego dedicated the gliderport to the "Youth of California" in 1939. Regional glider contests were held in 1939 and 1940, and the local glider pilots became so adept at their art that they invented new launch methods such as the "auto-tow pulley-tow takeoff," developed sensitive variometers (instruments to indicate rate of climb to the pilot), and took top honors at regional and national glider meets. John Robinson became America's first three-time national soaring champion, as well as first in the world to achieve soaring's highest honor, the Diamond C badge.

During World War II, the gliderport and its surrounds were turned into United States Army Camp Callan, an antiaircraft training facility. Thousands of troops trained at the base, preparing for duty and for a possible invasion of the west coast by the Japanese. The glider pilots who had learned to soar at Torrey Pines now instructed new glider pilots for war in the United States Army Air Corps at locations like Twentynine Palms, California, and Elmira, New York.

However, directly after the war, glider-minded San Diegans reopened the Torrey Pines Gliderport, and another new generation of pilots enjoyed the unique conditions that allow for silent flight. This new generation benefited from inexpensive gliders that were available as World War II surplus and from advancing thought in aerodynamics. Improved airfoils and construction methods allowed pilots to soar for significant distance, altitude, and duration. A new annual soaring contest was arranged for the gliderport: the Pacific Coast Midwinter Soaring Championships, the longest running glider contest held at one location in American history. Famous aviators such as Paul MacCready, Bill Ivans, Sterling Starr, Helen Dick, Paul Bikle, Richard Johnson, Gus Briegleb, and many others enjoyed these fun contests. The beauty of the site, the regular afternoon sea breezes, the cliffs providing lift, and the beach below for landings if the winds ebbed provided soaring's perfect playground. Postwar air-minded San Diegans turned out by the thousands on the weekends simply to watch these inspirational pilots soar effortlessly like birds. In turn, the pilots looked to Torrey Pines itself for their inspiration. Those like Paul MacCready developed a mantra of "doing more with less," devising increasingly efficient designs, and applying those lessons to engineering very broadly. The philosophy of efficiency, low power, and renewable energy led MacCready to develop the first human-powered aircraft to cross the English Channel, the first solar-powered aircraft to do the same, the aerodynamic EV-1 electric car for General Motors, and other inventions that together demonstrate the indelible mark that the Torrey Pines Gliderport has left on San Diego and technology in general.

Over time, other disciplines of gliding and soaring came to also realize that Torrey Pines is a special location for their own method of flight, a resource unlike any other. In the 1950s, radio-control enthusiasts began flying their model sailplanes from the cliffs. A world record of over eight hours was established in 1956 at Torrey Pines for this activity. In the 1970s, hang gliding enthusiasts took to the skies at Torrey Pines, first in their Rogallo wings, and later with ever more specialized designs for improved performance. Four world records for hang glider endurance were established at Torrey Pines, including the first flight of over one hour in a hang glider. In the 1990s, paragliders came on the scene, with their colorful airfoiled parachutes, maneuvered by a pilot seated below. All gliding disciplines share the resource with manned sailplanes, which continue to operate in the winter months. Together, these pilots consider the Torrey Pines Gliderport to be "Kitty Hawk of the West," a historic location that celebrates San Diego's 130-year fascination with gliding and aviation through a daily air show of silent flight.

One

Glider Pioneers

John Joseph Montgomery (1858–1911) is credited as the first American to pilot a heavier-than-air flying machine in a controlled fashion. Educated in physics, he experimented with a series of three successful manned gliders from 1884 to 1886 at Otay, California, just to the south of San Diego. His early interest in aerodynamics led to continued success with gliders for the remainder of his life, mainly in the San Francisco Bay area as a physics professor at Santa Clara College. (Courtesy of the San Diego Air and Space Museum.)

The Montgomery "Fruitland" ranch at Otay, California, served as the location where Montgomery built his gliders, with flights from surrounding hillsides. Montgomery was one of the earliest ornithologists in the area, studying soaring birds in great detail. He applied the lessons of their designs and mechanics to manned gliding flight. Montgomery also was the first to recognize that the confluence of daily afternoon sea breezes and sunshine in San Diego were perfect for gliding experiments. (Courtesy of the Bruce Coons Collection.)

Many aviation pioneers continued to rediscover San Diego's idyllic conditions for gliding between the 1900s and 1920s. Gliding was an inexpensive means to achieve flight. Donald Gordon (El Cajon), Waldo Waterman (San Diego), Frazier Curtis (La Jolla), A. Clare Rand (Escondido), Max Shemer and Maury Tombler (Point Loma), Elmore Shoudy (Bonita), and others experimented with hang gliders from the many hillsides. Octave Chanute, one of the fathers of American aviation, considered San Diego to be idyllic for gliding as early as 1894. When the Wright brothers wrote to him in 1900 asking for possible locations to test their flying machines, Chanute replied "the two most suitable locations for winter experiments which I know of are near San Diego, California, and St. James City (Pine Island), Florida, on account of the steady sea breezes which I have found to blow there." The Wright brothers selected Kitty Hawk, North Carolina, instead. (Courtesy of the San Diego Air and Space Museum.)

In 1927, William Hawley Bowlus worked as the superintendent of construction at San Diego's Ryan Aircraft Company during the construction of Charles Lindbergh's Ryan NYP *Spirit of St. Louis*. Bowlus had his own long-standing interest in gliders. By New Year's Day 1929, Bowlus completed construction of his 16th glider, the Bowlus S-16, the first true "sailplane" of American design and construction. His motorless aircraft was so efficient that in the right environmental conditions it could maintain or even gain altitude above its point of takeoff without the need of a motor. (Courtesy of the San Diego Air and Space Museum.)

The Bowlus S-16 sailplane debuted at the San Diego Air Service hangar on Lindbergh Field in 1929. The empty sailplane weighed only 160 pounds despite a wingspan of 44 feet. As part of the construction, Bowlus used craft paper for part of the wing ribs to reduce overall weight. As such, the aircraft became known as the *Paperwing*. It was the only Bowlus sailplane to use this method of construction. (Courtesy of the Gary Fogel Collection.)

Test flights of the *Paperwing* were made at Lindbergh Field and at Bonita using a car to tow the glider behind a rope for short glides. Lindbergh Field was only a few months old, a flat dirt landing strip by the harbor dedicated as San Diego's municipal airport. Bowlus later established the Bowlus Sailplane Company and taught students to fly gliders at the Bowlus Glider School at Lindbergh Field. (Courtesy of the Gary Fogel Collection.)

The first glider meet in San Diego was held in Pacific Beach on July 4–5, 1929, and was arranged by the Pacific Beach Business Men's Association and the San Diego Chamber of Commerce. Launches were made from a 350-foot hill on the south slope of Mount Soledad. Entrants came from all over Southern California to compete with their designs. Many flew primary gliders like this one piloted by Bill Atwood from Riverside, launched from the side of the mountain by bungee cord. Later in his life, Atwood became well known as a producer of model aircraft engines. Other young entrants went on to fabulous careers in aviation and science including Apollo Smith (who subsequently became a fixture at Douglas Aircraft and helped design the jet assisted takeoff—or JATO—system), Irv Culver (who later helped design the Lockheed P-38 Lightning and Constellation and coined the term "Skunk Works"), and John Pierce (who later supervised the Bell Laboratories team that developed the transistor, and the first commercial communications satellite—*Telstar 1*). The burgeoning sport of gliding held a particular fascination with Southern California's air-minded youth. (Courtesy of the Gary Fogel Collection.)

Bowlus entered his *Paperwing* sailplane at the local glider meet, capturing the duration category with a flight of 1 minute and 45 seconds and the distance category with a flight of three quarters of a mile. A second glider meet was held at Pacific Beach in September 1929 with Bowlus again taking top honors. Interest in his graceful sailplane grew rapidly, and many spectators came to witness flying machines that could fly like birds without any propellers. (Courtesy of the San Diego Air and Space Museum.)

Bowlus recognized that his sailplane could be used to establish new gliding endurance records. His legendary ridge soaring flights along the promontory of Point Loma in 1929 and 1930 pushed the American soaring endurance mark from minutes, to one hour, to over nine hours. These daring accomplishments made national headlines, and were especially uplifting during the height of the Great Depression. (Courtesy of the Gary Fogel Collection.)

Upon hearing of Bowlus's record soaring flights, Charles Lindbergh (below, right) returned to San Diego in January 1930 specifically to receive glider instruction from Bowlus (left). Lindbergh learned to soar in Bowlus sailplanes at Point Loma; soon thereafter, Bowlus and Lindbergh surveyed locations throughout California in hopes of extended duration and distance flights. Point Loma continued to attract local glider enthusiasts such as Alan "Dick" Essery, Forrest Hieatt, Earle Mitchell, Bud Perl, William Beuby, Lowell Bullen, Albert Hastings, I.N. Lawson, Allison Moore, William Van Dusen, Dr. H. Karl William Kumm, Sterling Owen, Robert Goebel, Al Gabbs, and many others. (Courtesy of the San Diego Air and Space Museum.)

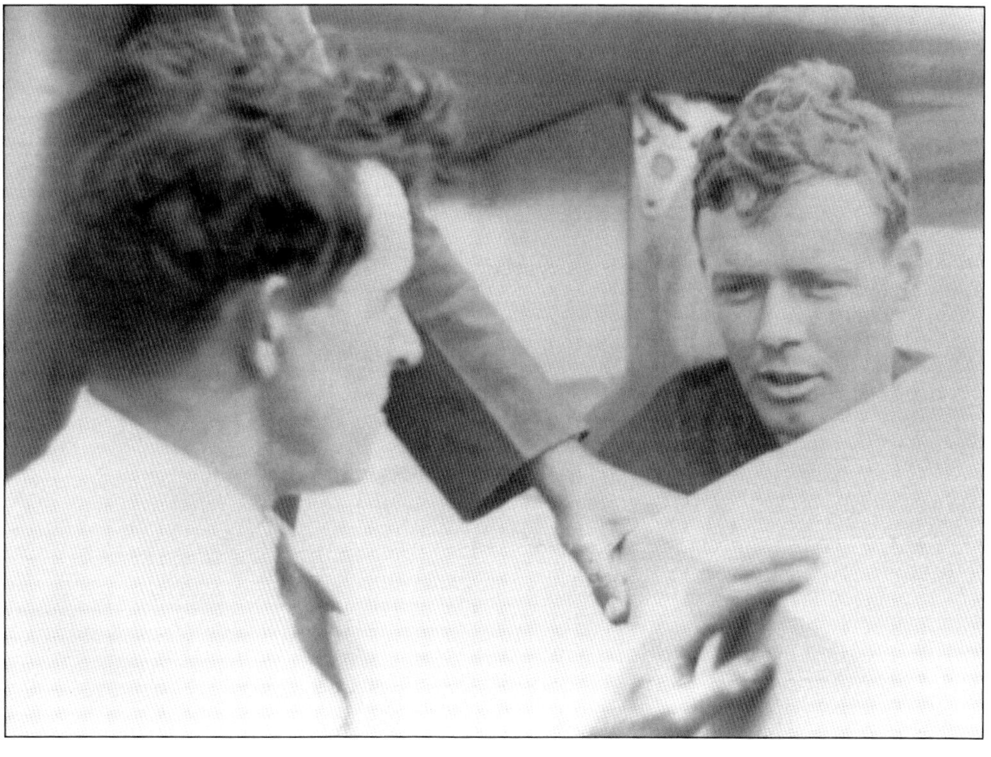

Under the leadership of Dr. H. Karl William Kumm of Pacific Beach, the Associated Glider Clubs of Southern California was formed in 1929. Glider clubs from all across Southern California came together under this organization to help preserve glider sites and arrange contests. Mount Soledad in La Jolla was selected as the club's primary glider base. Dr. Kumm was a noted scientist and explorer, reportedly one of the first Caucasians to traverse the area between the Congo and the Nile in Africa. (Courtesy of the San Diego Air and Space Museum.)

Also interested in soaring, on January 29, 1930, Anne Lindbergh completed her introductory gliding lesson using a primary glider towed behind a car at Lindbergh Field. That same afternoon, Anne was launched in a Bowlus sailplane from the top of Mount Soledad, resulting in a flight of over six minutes. This single flight qualified Anne for her third-class, second-class, and first-class glider licenses. She was the first woman in the United States to achieve the first-class glider license (Maxine Dunlap of San Francisco predated her with a third-class license). Anne's widely publicized achievement helped open the sport of gliding to women. The Anne Lindbergh Gliders Club, composed of 23 women, formed within one month and began taking lessons at the Bowlus Glider School. Anne Lindbergh was made an honorary member. (Courtesy of the San Diego Air and Space Museum.)

Anne Lindbergh is in the cockpit of the 60-foot wingspan Bowlus Model A sailplane with the launch crew preparing for their effort. Charles Lindbergh waits patiently nearest Anne, while Hawley Bowlus walks behind the aircraft, double checking the scene. (Courtesy of the San Diego Air and Space Museum.)

Anne Lindbergh is being launched into the sky from Mount Soledad. Rather than having conventional ailerons, the large Bowlus sailplanes used tip ailerons to provide roll control. (Courtesy of the San Diego Air and Space Museum.)

Members of the Anne Lindbergh Gliders Club began their training with the Bowlus Glider School at Lindbergh Field, making gliding flights at other locations in San Diego including Mount Soledad and Morena. Three members in particular excelled at the sport. Peaches Wallace, Ruth Alexander, and Ellen Guinivere "Gwen" Kotter all qualified for third-class and second-class glider licenses. Ruth Alexander went on to establish several records in light powered planes including a flight to 26,600 feet in the skies above San Diego. She also became the first woman glider instructor in the United States. (Courtesy of the Gary Fogel Collection.)

On the afternoon of February 24, 1930, Charles Lindbergh was launched from Mount Soledad in a new Bowlus sailplane S-20 that was owned by the Anne Lindbergh Gliders Club named *The Good Ship Anne*. Following launch, Lindbergh continued soaring to the north, over La Jolla Shores, and to the ridge lift provided by the steep cliffs at Torrey Pines and the prevailing westerly sea breeze. Lindbergh was the first to recognize and make use of the lift at this location. (Courtesy of the San Diego Air and Space Museum.)

Lindbergh continued on his soaring path, including the full length of the cliffs at Torrey Pines, past the Torrey Pines Lodge, to a soft landing on the beach near Del Mar. Curious onlookers stopped their cars in amazement, witnessing the large aircraft that apparently had made an emergency landing as it had obviously lost its propeller. They were even more shocked when none other than Lucky Lindy emerged from the cockpit, signaling that everything was fine. The flight was immediately hailed as a western regional distance record. Lindbergh was quoted as saying, "I see a great future for gliding in America. It will sweep the country during 1930 and I expect to see a million glider pilots within the next three years." (Courtesy of the Gary Fogel Collection.)

The publicity associated with the Lindberghs' gliding accomplishments helped introduce a new generation of young male and female aviators to the sport, and heightened interest in Bowlus sailplanes. (Courtesy of the Gary Fogel Collection.)

Bowlus and Charles Lindbergh surveyed much of California for suitable soaring sites, including locations at Lebec and Carmel. Unfortunately, the winds were uncooperative and no records for gliding endurance were established by Lindbergh, despite several attempts with *The Good Ship Anne*. (Courtesy of the Gary Fogel Collection.)

Sixteen-year-old Bud Perl assisted with glider instruction at the Bowlus Glider School, pictured here with the primary glider *Tillie the Toiler*. This same aircraft was used to provide initial instruction to Anne Lindbergh prior to her soaring flight. Bud Perl maintained an active interest in gliding in San Diego for many years, flying at both Point Loma and the Torrey Pines Gliderport through the mid-1930s. (Courtesy of the Gary Fogel Collection.)

Two

A Gliderport is Born

Harland Ross was trained as an aviation mechanic at North Island Naval Air Station, San Diego, and became quite interested in Bowlus's glider activities. Earning his glider rating at the Bowlus Glider School while still enlisted with the Navy, Ross designed and built his first sailplane, the Ross R-1000 *Silver King*. This sailplane was test flown on the beach at the north end of the Torrey Pines cliffs in November 1930 with several ridge soaring flights of limited duration following car tow. Over the next three decades, Ross forged an incredible legacy of American sailplane design, resulting in many sailplanes that established national and world records. (Courtesy of the Soaring Society of America.)

Harland Ross is soaring in the *Silver King* at Torrey Pines in late 1930. (Courtesy of the Gary Fogel Collection.)

Students at many local high schools convinced their woodshop instructors to build gliders instead of chairs or boats. San Diego High School students were particularly fortunate to have aviation-minded Letain Kittredge as their woodshop teacher. Kittredge had served as a Naval aviator at North Island during World War I. Woodshop students completed their gliders at school and then flew them from various locations in San Diego. One favorite of San Diego High School students was to tow their gliders aloft with a car (an "auto-tow") from the beach at the north end of the Torrey Pines cliffs. Student Mary Wind (left) and instructor Roland Fetters are pictured here in a specially designed, oversized, two-place primary glider used specifically for flight instruction. After releasing from the tow rope, the updraft from the cliffs provided sufficient lift for soaring, with landings made back on the beach below. Fetters, David Roberson, Vincent Loop, and Ernie Stout were the primary instructors as they had accumulated the most air time. (Courtesy of the Soaring Society of America.)

One graduate of San Diego High School, John Robinson, became particularly enamored with silent flight. He also excelled at welding, and began designing and constructing his own steel tube sailplane fuselages. Robinson evaluated many of these designs—first on the beach below the cliffs at Torrey Pines, and then later off the tops of the cliffs. (Courtesy of the Soaring Society of America.)

Pictured here is Robinson's *Robin No. 1* on the beach near the Torrey Pines Grade around 1934. Robinson decided to make a series of Robins all based on this first one. There were five Robins in all, including the original. (Courtesy of the National Soaring Museum.)

Woodbridge "Woody" Brown came west from New York to La Jolla with prior experience in gliding. With an interest in surfing, he quickly learned of the San Diego High School students flying their gliders on the beach near Torrey Pines. He purchased Henry Severin and David Robertson's *Swift* sailplane. Here, Woody Brown (right) prepares the *Swift* for auto-tow takeoff from the beach around 1935. The hard packed sand made a perfect runway, although shoreline fishermen were less than pleased with the gliding activities. (Courtesy of the Gary Fogel Collection.)

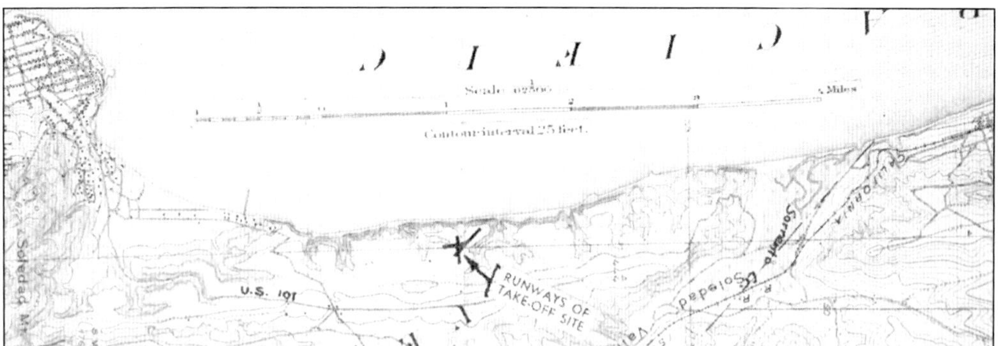

To avoid issues with the fishermen and tides, operations were moved to the tops of the cliffs in 1936, giving rise to the Torrey Pines Gliderport. This map from the period in *Soaring* magazine shows three runways at the gliderport including a main west-to-east runway, a diagonal northwest runway, and a third south-to-north runway. The beach below was still used for landings when winds subsided prematurely, although retrieval from the beach south of Bathtub Rock or north of the Scripps Pier was difficult unless at low tide. Woody Brown became the first to successfully launch and land on top of the cliffs, using the *Swift* sailplane. (Courtesy of the Soaring Society of America.)

While soaring along the cliffs towards the south in 1937, one could see the three runways that comprised the gliderport when looking east. The line of trees on the horizon marked US Highway 101. In 1937, the Associated Glider Clubs of Southern California obtained a five-year lease for the property from the City of San Diego for glider operations at $50 per year. (Courtesy of the Soaring Society of America.)

Woody Brown and John Robinson enjoyed many paired soaring flights along the Torrey Pines cliffs in the 1930s. This photograph from 1937 shows Robinson soaring in a v as viewed from Woody's *Swift* with the pier from the Scripps Institution of Oceanography and La Jolla in the distance. Given the daily westerly sea breeze, soaring was possible along the full length of the cliffs, a distance of roughly four miles. However, in 1937, the US Bureau of Air Commerce prohibited the flying of unlicensed aircraft in federal airways throughout the United States. The gliderport was located within the airway between San Diego and Los Angeles. Woody Brown and other club members mounted a campaign to have the gliderport become the first and only location in America with a special exemption to this rule, specifically so that the young pilots could continue their experimentation with sailplanes. (Courtesy of the Soaring Society of America.)

Soaring towards the north, John Robinson captured this aerial photograph of the steep coastal cliffs in 1937. Woody Brown made an endurance flight at Torrey of nine hours in the *Swift* during 1938. When the winds were uncooperative, Woody spent his free time surfing. He became one of the first surfers to use the break at Windansea in La Jolla. He also applied his knowledge of glider construction to build pioneering hollow plywood surfboards in 1936. In the surfing community he became known as "Spider" for his unusual stance while surfing. He became well known in both sports. (Courtesy of the Soaring Society of America.)

This is the first club logo for the Associated Glider Clubs of Southern California. (Courtesy of the Gary Fogel Collection.)

John Robinson takes off in a Robin sailplane via auto-tow. Standard automobiles were used to do the towing, although after a rain, stopping the car in the muddy terrain before the cliff edge presented its own level of excitement. (Courtesy of the Soaring Society of America.)

The Robin designs incorporated see-through nose panels, providing exceptional forward visibility for landing. Robinson is shown here after a cross-country flight from Torrey Pines to a landing near Alpine, California, in 1939. The glider pilots at Torrey became proficient at reading both the lift on the ridge and also passing thermals (columns of rising air), circling in them and climbing to great heights before soaring east to find the next thermal and continue their journey. Robinson, Alan "Dick" Essery, and Brown made exceptional cross-country flights from Torrey Pines. Robinson set a US altitude record of over 7,600 feet in the *Robin No. 3* from Clark Dry Lake near Borrego, clearing the Santa Rosa Mountains along the way. (Courtesy of Soaring Society of America.)

Dick Essery developed his own series of primary gliders in the 1920s and 1930s, flying them from many locations in San Diego. Essery was a steady enthusiastic force behind gliding in Southern California and served as president of the Associated Glider Clubs of Southern California in the late 1930s. (Courtesy of the Soaring Society of America.)

Many other pilots from the San Diego area used Torrey Pines for soaring. For example, Steve Kesckes (pictured), who had flown gliders from the beach in the early 1930s, purchased the *Sloanlo* secondary glider from Jay Buxton in Los Angeles. "Slow and low" was a perfect description of its flight characteristics, as it would soar gently on the updrafts. (Courtesy of the Doug Fronius Collection.)

Bud Perl and William "Bill" Beuby modified an early Bowlus sailplane and used it for soaring at Torrey Pines. Both Perl and Beuby had soared at Point Loma with Bowlus in 1930. In June 1932, they launched the sailplane by auto-tow at La Jolla Shores, continuing to Del Mar and back again. In this photograph from around 1935, Perl is in the cockpit of their modified Bowlus sailplane while Beuby stands outside. Together, they helped form the San Diego Soaring Society, which for a time was also located, with the Associated Glider Clubs of Southern California, at Torrey Pines. Perl continued his interest in aviation, working at the Van Bezel Sailplane Company, then Solar Aircraft, Lockheed Aircraft, and General Dynamics (Convair) until his retirement. Beuby continued soaring into the 1950s, receiving the Barringer Trophy from the Soaring Society of America for the longest soaring flight of 1951 (141.5 miles). Beuby was also on the US team that attended the World Soaring Championships in 1952. (Courtesy of the Gary Fogel Collection.)

Carl Goller prepares to launch his *Goller Sailplane* for a test flight in late 1936 on the beach via auto-tow slightly north of Torrey Pines State Park. Goller worked for Ryan Aircraft and his sailplane was constructed with the assistance of George Palmer and Vernon Yates. (Courtesy of the San Diego Air and Space Museum.)

The *Goller Sailplane* is pictured on auto-tow at Torrey Pines. Goller built the sailplane with the specific purpose of setting world records for soaring endurance and also interesting the citizens of San Diego in the sport of soaring. (Courtesy of the Soaring Society of America.)

Carl Goller is about to release from auto-tow as he begins his soaring journey out over the cliffs and Pacific Ocean below. Once the sailplanes had cleared the edge, upward lifting currents of air awaited and ridge soaring was possible. (Courtesy of the San Diego Air and Space Museum.)

Like many other local glider pilots involved with the local aviation industry, Jerry Litell worked as a machine shop inspector at Consolidated Aircraft Corporation. Litell made a series of sailplanes such as this one shown taking off at Torrey Pines via auto-tow around 1936. Litell helped advertise the Torrey Pines Gliderport with his pen, authoring many articles describing the beauty and grace of silent flight. (Courtesy of the San Diego Air and Space Museum.)

S.D. Soaring Club To Dedicate Field At Torrey Pines

By GENE STECK

THEY'LL DO TRICKS AT 300 FEET NEW YEAR'S DAY

From December 31, 1938, through January 2, 1939, a three-day glider meet was planned for the gliderport. San Diego mayor Percy J. Benbough dedicated the property to the youth of California for the purpose of gliding. More than 1,000 spectators came to watch the activities as entrants competed for the Bishop Trophy. Despite poor soaring conditions, flights were made by Robinson, Hawley Bowlus, Frank Wolcott, Bob Heideman, Ray Parker, and others. John Robinson took top honors as meet champion. (Courtesy of the Gary Fogel Collection.)

Shortly after the dedication ceremonies, John Robinson launched in his Robin with 295 pieces of cacheted (and an additional 50 pieces of uncacheted) glider mail. La Jolla postmaster Nathan Rannells awaited his landing. One envelope was forwarded to President Roosevelt while another was forwarded to the director of the National Youth Administration. Nathan Rannells also had his own experience with gliders, having helped Frazier Curtis make the first glider flights in La Jolla with a Chanute-type hang glider in 1910. (Courtesy of the Gary Fogel Collection.)

In 1939, with a large loan from club member Ernie Stout, the Associated Glider Clubs of Southern California purchased this two-place Grunau 8 sailplane as its official club sailplane for dual instruction. The sailplane was originally built by David Sanborn of Redlands, California, in 1936 and had spent time with a club in San Francisco prior to coming to San Diego. With this sailplane, membership in the club grew steadily. Club soaring instructors included Alan Essery, Woody Brown, Frank Graham, and Ray and Harry Parker. (Courtesy of the Soaring Society of America.)

Dick Essery (left) and John Robinson stand next to a Robin sailplane while enjoying springtime soaring at the annual Western Soaring Championships at Arvin, California, near Bakersfield. After honing their skills at Torrey Pines, Essery, Robinson, Brown, and Ray Parker became a tour de force at regional and national contests. (Courtesy of the Soaring Society of America.)

Woody Brown spent hours soaring at Torrey in his *Swift* and later this Bowlus Baby Albatross nicknamed the *Thunder Bird*. At the Southwest Soaring Contest held at Wichita Falls, Texas, on June 6, 1939, Brown and the *Thunder Bird* completed a 280-mile goal distance flight from Wichita Falls to Wichita, Kansas, for a new American record. Crossing three states to land at a previously declared goal in a sailplane was considered so impressive that Brown received a hero's welcome upon his return to Wichita Falls, including a parade and a congratulatory telegram from President Roosevelt, and even was later featured in a *Ripley's Believe it or Not!* comic. (Courtesy of the Soaring Society of America.)

As a result of his record flight, Brown made the cover of *Soaring* magazine in July 1939. He also went on to take top honors at the third annual Western Championship Soaring Contest held at Arvin, California, in 1940. He moved to Hawaii shortly thereafter, and became one of the first Caucasians to surf the big waves on Oahu's north shore at Waimea Bay. The surfing spot known as "Woody's" near Lahiana, Maui, is named in his honor. After World War II, Woody designed and built the first modern catamaran, the *Manu Kai*, offering rides to tourists from the beach at Waikiki. His *Manu Kai* led directly to the popular catamaran developed by Hobie Alter—the Hobie Cat. (Courtesy of the Soaring Society of America.)

Dick Essery (right) also enjoyed championships of his own, taking first place at the fourth annual Western Championships at Arvin, California, in his two-place sailplane named the *Baby Bomber*. (Courtesy of the Soaring Society of America.)

Essery properly tuned his *Baby Bomber* through hours of soaring at the Torrey Pines Gliderport. The *Bomber* was constructed of Bowlus Baby Albatross wings and a specially designed side-by-side two-place fuselage, which made the fuselage wider than most sailplanes. Many of Essery's friends had their first taste of soaring in this sailplane including engineers from local aviation firms, who signed up for glider lessons with the Associated Glider Clubs of Southern California shortly thereafter. (Courtesy of the Gary Fogel Collection.)

The Bowlus Baby Albatross was offered as a kit to glider enthusiasts for $425. Hawley Bowlus continued designing gliders throughout the 1930s and 1940s, and even used his deep knowledge of aerodynamics to design the Bowlus Road Chief, the predecessor to the more famous Airstream road trailer. (Courtesy of Soaring Society of America.)

In March 1940, a second Torrey Pines glider meet was held including many entrants and spectators from all over San Diego. Many pilots flew the popular Bowlus sailplanes including a Bowlus Super Albatross (foreground), which awaits takeoff behind a trio of Bowlus Baby Albatrosses. Parked near the cars in the distance, the club Grunau 8 sailplane awaits passengers. Reuben H. Fleet, the owner of the Consolidated Aircraft Company, demonstrated a keen interest in the gliding activities at Torrey Pines and donated the three first prizes for competitions at the meet. John Robinson repeated as meet champion. (Courtesy of the Gary Fogel Collection.)

Harvey Stephens (in the cockpit of the *Thunder Bird*) also attended the 1940 Torrey Pines meet. Stephens was a Hollywood actor who took a great interest in soaring. He had commissioned Harland Ross to design a gull-winged sailplane for him, the *R.S.-1* (Ross-Stephens 1). Stephens eventually traded the *R.S.-1* to Woody Brown for the *Thunder Bird* after damaging the *R.S.-1* in a contest. Brown repaired the *R.S.-1* and then sold it to John Robinson, who renamed it the *Zanonia*. (Courtesy of the Soaring Society of America.)

The *Thunder Bird* was later purchased from Stephens by the Associated Glider Clubs of Southern California as a single-place club ship. Ernie Stout, Scott Royce, and Jerry Litell were responsible for the arrangements. Following instruction in the Grunau 8, the *Thunder Bird* was used for hours of solo flight. In this photograph, club member Jim Spurgeon prepares for a takeoff at Torrey Pines. (Courtesy of the Gary Fogel Collection.)

In 1938, members of the Crown City Glider Club Walter Burke, Irv Culver, and Wallace Neugent designed and built the *Screamin' Wiener*. The *Wiener* was a very small sailplane, limited to a 36-foot wingspan because of the garage used during construction. Ray Parker flew the *Wiener* at the 1940 Torrey Pines meet and placed second with it at the 1946 National Soaring Contest. It was sold to Paul MacCready, who also placed second with it at the 1947 National Soaring Contest. At the 1947 meet, MacCready set a goal and return world record of 230 miles in the *Wiener*. (Courtesy of the Gary Fogel Collection.)

Three

Camp Callan

Given the likelihood of impending war, at the request of the US Army, the City of San Diego and other local property owners leased roughly 1,200 acres (including the Torrey Pines Gliderport) to the Army for the purpose of building a Coast Artillery Replacement Training Center. Construction of Camp Callan began in November 1940, and the base was officially occupied January 15, 1941. The camp was named after Maj. Gen. Robert E. Callan (1874–1936), a veteran of the Spanish-American War and World War I and one of the most distinguished officers in the history of the Coast Artillery. The main entrance was located near the present-day Torrey Pines Golf Course to the north of the gliderport. (Courtesy of the Judy Schulman Collection.)

An aerial view of the southern half of US Army Camp Callan shows barracks covering the area just to the east of the gliderport property, with Mount Soledad in the distance. (Courtesy of the Gary Fogel Collection.)

When viewed to the west, the open spaces of the gliderport were transformed into physical training facilities including an obstacle course, ammunition magazines, plotting rooms, a plant nursery, and areas for artillery emplacements. (Courtesy of the Judy Schulman Collection.)

Ironically, Camp Callan focused on antiaircraft artillery training, with a secondary purpose of coastal defense in preparation for a Japanese assault on the west coast. Ninety-millimeter gun emplacements were established along the cliff edge, with crews firing their guns at 10-foot sleeves towed behind powered aircraft. The battery pictured here was stationed at the far north end of the gliderport in November 1942, just to the west of the diagonal runway. La Jolla and Mount Soledad are pictured in the distance. (Courtesy of the Judy Schulman Collection.)

Batteries of 155-millimeter Howitzers on the gliderport practiced firing towards the Pacific Ocean. While the initial emphasis of the camp focused on antiaircraft and coast artillery, by March 1942, a decision was made to focus solely on antiaircraft training. This led to a rapid buildup of Camp Callan, with 15,000 enlisted men iteratively going through 13-week training cycles. Separate ranges were established at Camp Callan for pistols, rifles, automatic weapons, and larger antiaircraft artillery. (Courtesy of the Judy Schulman Collection.)

In January 1943, S.Sgt. Woodrow Ulm (kneeling) invented a visual training device to help direct antiaircraft fire. Here, he explains the approach to other servicemen at Camp Callan. The chart on the left was used to track the course of different aircraft, while the device on the right was used to illustrate possible firing options. (Courtesy of the Judy Schulman Collection.)

Brig. Gen. Francis P. Hardaway (left), Camp Callan's first commanding officer, met Maj. Gen. W.E. Smith (right) of the Marine Corps at Camp Callan on February 27, 1943. Major General Smith led a demonstration of the Marine Tank Corps for the troops at Camp Callan. (Courtesy of the Judy Schulman Collection.)

Loud booms from Camp Callan were audible in La Jolla on a daily basis. The irony of the Torrey Pines Gliderport being converted into an antiaircraft facility was not lost on local glider pilots, many of whom were either employed in local aviation companies in support of the war effort, or volunteered at locations across the nation as instructors in support of glider training programs for the US Army Air Corps. (Courtesy of the Judy Schulman Collection.)

By December 1943, Camp Callan had grown to include its own hospital, five post exchanges, two indoor theaters, three chapels, many support and storage buildings, and even a very large outdoor theater with seating for 5,000. The theater was slightly to the northeast of the gliderport. To the left of the theater, behind the grove of eucalyptus trees, was a large post exchange warehouse. The foundation of this post exchange warehouse remains to the present day as a tie-down pad for gliders, the largest remaining aspect of Camp Callan. (Courtesy of Judy Schulman Collection.)

Camp Callan troops make their way through a series of obstacles on the grounds of the gliderport. (Courtesy of the Gary Fogel Collection.)

The official mascot of the Coast Artillery Corps was the Oozlefinch, a legendary bird that reportedly flew backward in order to keep the dust out of its eyes. (Courtesy of the Gary Fogel Collection.)

Four

Gliding Returns to Torrey Pines

During World War II, the US Navy prohibited civilian aircraft flights within 150 miles of the Pacific coastline. No coastal gliding flights were possible. However, in 1945, Camp Callan was decommissioned and the Navy prohibition was lifted. Local glider fans acted quickly to renew their lease for the Torrey Pines Gliderport with the City of San Diego in 1946. Glider runways were remarked and graded, including a runway for takeoff (left) and a runway for landing (right). The diagonal runway was also restored. (Courtesy of the Gary Fogel Collection.)

For a few years after the war, the Associated Glider Clubs of Southern California maintained its clubhouse in one of the leftover Quonset huts from Camp Callan that was previously used as an ammunition magazine. Pictured here is a young military cadet examining a model of an early Montgomery glider that was used to help explain the history of gliding to San Diegans at this clubhouse. (Courtesy of the Gary Fogel Collection.)

The original Associated Glider Clubs of Southern California winch was mounted securely to the back of this truck and stationed on the hill at the west end of the gliderport. Winch operators worked inside the large metal cage for safety in the unlikely event of a cable break. A specially devised guillotine could also be used to slice the cable and set the glider free in the event of a mechanical issue. This winch was used in various configurations by the Associated Glider Clubs of Southern California for decades. (Courtesy of the Gary Fogel Collection.)

Henrietta Kecskes served as the president of the Associated Glider Clubs of Southern California in 1946, helping to reopen the gliderport with her husband, Steve Kecskes, among others. (Courtesy of the Andy Kecskes Collection.)

Robert "Bob" Fronius was an experienced pilot and parachutist who along with Wally Wiberg attempted to set a two-place sailplane endurance record at Torrey Pines shortly after the gliderport reopened. Fronius was also the first to demonstrate the in-air recovery of an aircraft (a Robin sailplane) using a large parachute, an aviation feat he completed at the 1949 Torrey Pines meet. (Courtesy of the Doug Fronius Collection.)

Jim Spurgeon is pictured with his Frankfort Cinema (TG-1A) *Duchess*, preparing for a winch launch. Spurgeon became the historian for the Associated Glider Clubs of Southern California, collecting information on regional gliding history going back to John J. Montgomery. He helped lead various efforts to work with the media and popularize not only Torrey Pines, but also Montgomery's role in the history of American aviation. (Courtesy of the Gary Fogel Collection.)

The Schweizer SGS 2-8 was used throughout the United States for glider training during World War II. After the war, surplus gliders such as these were sold at exceptionally low prices to civilians. In this photograph, Associated Glider Clubs of Southern California member Harry Parker examines the club Schweizer SGS 2-8 before a flight. (Courtesy of the Gary Fogel Collection.)

DeVaughn North enjoys a long excursion over the cliffs of Torrey Pines in the club SGS 2-8. Club members commonly referred to this sailplane as a TG-2 despite it actually being one of the less common LNS-1 varieties of the SGS 2-8 used by the Marines during the war. (Courtesy of the Soaring Society of America.)

The Associated Glider Clubs of Southern California advertised the first annual Pacific Coast Midwinter Soaring Championships to be held at Torrey Pines in January 1947. A new trophy was offered: the John J. Montgomery Memorial Championship Trophy. Ray Parker (pictured in cockpit) entered his *Rigid Midget* sailplane in the 1947 Torrey Pines glider meet. Herman Stiglmeier was the first to win the trophy as meet champion. (Courtesy of the Gary Fogel Collection.)

John Robinson became America's first three-time national soaring champion (1940, 1941, and 1946) in his *Zanonia*. Robinson relocated to Los Angeles after the war. As a member of the Southern California Soaring Association, he flew the *Zanonia* at locations all across California and the nation. (Courtesy of Gary Fogel Collection.)

Associated Glider Clubs of Southern California vice president Charles Rowen demonstrates the best way to attach the winch line to the Schweizer TG-2 for local ladies (and the cameras) at the 1948 Torrey Pines meet. (Courtesy of the Soaring Society of America.)

Winners of the 1948 Torrey Pines meet are pictured here, including, from left to right, Herman Stiglmeier, Paul Tuntland, Richard Johnson, John Robinson, Gus Briegleb, and Joe Stasnick. (Courtesy of the Soaring Society of America.)

Richard "Dick" Johnson launches at the 1948 Torrey Pines Meet via winch in a Schweizer TG-2 in an attempt for a cross-country flight. He managed to find a thermal near the gliderport, and soared from there in a southeasterly direction. At an altitude of just 600 feet above La Mesa, he encountered another stronger thermal that took him to over 4,000 feet and he continued on. Three hours and one minute after takeoff, he finally landed in Tecate, Mexico. It was the first international glider flight from the United States, and was enough to capture the Montgomery Trophy as meet champion. Dick Johnson later became an 11-time United States National Soaring Champion, logging over 14,000 flying hours as one of America's most celebrated soaring pilots. (Courtesy of the Soaring Society of America.)

Perhaps the most iconic image in the history of the gliderport is this flyby featuring (from left to right) Gus Briegleb flying a Briegleb BG-7, Myron Wells in a Bowlus Super Albatross, Paul MacCready flying the gull-winged Orlik II, and John Robinson flying in the *Zanonia*. Over 12,000 spectators were treated to views such as this during the two-day Pacific Coast Midwinter Soaring Championships of 1949. Only two years after operations resumed at Torrey Pines, the Associated Glider Clubs of Southern California boasted 60 active members, with over 100 other associated members, five club sailplanes including two Schweizer TG-2s, a Frankfort TG-1, a Briegleb BG-7, and a Pratt-Read PR-G1 (TG-32). The annual meets were cooperatively organized with the San Diego Junior Chamber of Commerce and filmed by Fox Movietone News cameramen. MacCready was meet champion in 1949. (Courtesy of Soaring Society of America.)

Myron Wells makes a high-speed pass by the spectators in his Bowlus Super Albatross with Paul MacCready soaring in the Orlik II in the bottom left corner of the photograph. (Courtesy of the San Diego Air and Space Museum.)

CATCH THAT THERMAL

with a

ROBINSON VARIOMETER

(Pellet Type)

"No lag" feature tells immediately whether you are climbing or sinking

Two Models Available

Simplified Model

Without Air Chamber........................$25.00

DeLuxe Calibrated Model

With Insulated Air Chamber............$49.50

The New National Distance Record of 333 Miles was set by John Robinson using this Deluxe Model of the Robinson Rate-of-Climb Indicator.

Write for Descriptive Details

JOHN ROBINSON

254 South Rosemead Blvd.

Pasadena 10, Calif.

John Robinson developed a very sensitive pellet-type variometer (an instrument to indicate rate of climb to the pilot) and sold them nationally to sailplane pilots. Robinson calibrated each of the quite advanced Deluxe models individually while soaring in the *Zanonia* at Torrey Pines. (Courtesy of the Soaring Society of America.)

In this photograph, Myron Wells hugs the ridge in his Bowlus Super Albatross searching for lift with La Jolla Cove in the distance. As the sea breeze hits the cliff, it is forced upward like an inverted waterfall of rising air, providing a zone of constant lift for glider pilots. The rare combination of high coastal cliffs, a regular afternoon sea breeze, and the superior weather of San Diego made the Torrey Pines Gliderport a unique national treasure for ridge soaring. (Courtesy of the Gary Fogel Collection.)

Paul MacCready launches in his gull-winged Orlik II at Torrey Pines via winch as a part of the 1949 glider meet. MacCready won the meet with a five-hour cross-country flight to San Marcos. (Courtesy of the Gary Fogel Collection.)

MacCready enjoyed soaring in the ocean air at Torrey with the canopy purposefully removed. He established an American altitude record in the Orlik II on December 31, 1938, soaring to 29,500 feet over the Sierra Nevada Mountains. John Robinson eclipsed MacCready's mark on the very next day, January 1, 1939, with a flight to 33,500 feet in the *Zanonia*. MacCready and Robinson had a friendly rivalry in their gull-winged sailplanes, with MacCready becoming the next three-time national soaring champion (1948, 1949, and 1953) after Robinson. MacCready also became the first American to win the World Soaring Championship in 1956. (Courtesy of the Tyler MacCready Collection.)

John Robinson is flying in the *Zanonia* on the cliffs of Torrey Pines at the Pacific Coast Midwinter Soaring Championships. The gull-winged *Zanonia* was always a crowd pleaser. On one flight from winch launch, Robinson was able to soar along the cliffs to the north, all the way to a landing on the beach near Oceanside. In 1950, Robinson became the first sailplane pilot in the world to achieve soaring's highest achievement award, the Diamond C badge. The badge required a flight of over 310.7 miles, altitude gain of over 16,405 feet, and goal flight of over 186.42 miles. Robinson satisfied all three of these accomplishments in the *Zanonia*. (Courtesy of the San Diego Air and Space Museum.)

Ray Parker entered the *Rigid Midget* sailplane in the 1949 Torrey Pines meet. Parker was another exceptional pilot from the area, who also assisted as a glider instructor during World War II at Twentynine Palms. He captured the fourth Diamond C in the United States in 1952 and became a director of the Soaring Society of America. He is pictured here at the 1947 National Soaring Contest at Wichita Falls, Texas. (Courtesy of the Soaring Society of America.)

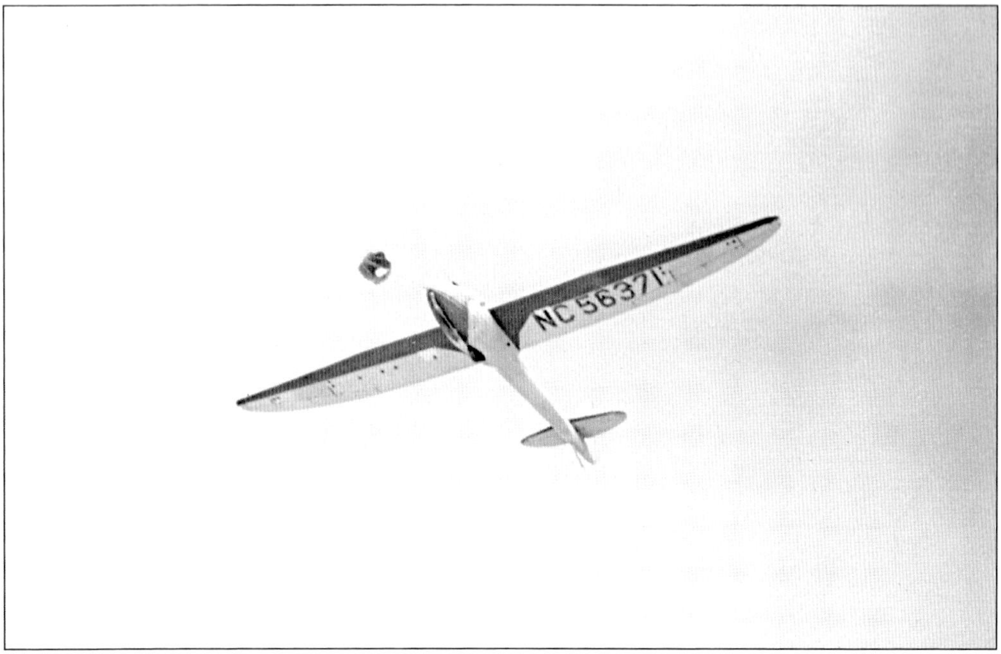

Herman Stiglmeier's Pratt-Read PR-G1 sailplane takes to the skies on the winch at Torrey Pines. The Pratt-Read was a two-place side-by-side training glider originally built by the Pratt-Read Piano Company for the military during the war. In 1948, Herman and his brother Henry established a new American endurance record for two-place gliders of 12 hours and 52 minutes soaring in this Pratt-Read over the Palos Verdes hills near Los Angeles. (Courtesy of the Gary Fogel Collection.)

Downwind landings at Torrey Pines were common given the lengthy rollout area to the east. Here, Stiglmeier lands the Pratt-Read to the east, crossing over the diagonal runway with a Navy calibration tower in the distance. The calibration tower was installed in 1934 along with a duplicate tower one nautical mile to the north. Ships at sea calibrated their equipment using the towers. (Courtesy of the Gary Fogel Collection.)

Five

The 1950s

San Diegans turned out in droves to watch the glider pilots soar effortlessly like giant birds at Torrey Pines. The Torrey Pines meets became an annual San Diego tradition and boosted interest in soaring. At Torrey, spectators could observe gliding and soaring up close. Pilots would make low passes and tight turns for the crowds, as shown by this pilot in his Bowlus Baby Albatross at the fourth annual Pacific Coast Midwinter Soaring Championships in 1950. (Courtesy of the Soaring Society of America.)

Gaggles of gliders soared back and forth along the coastline, remaining in the lifting zone provided by the cliff. Pilots obeyed specific ridge rules to enhance safety. Six sailplanes are shown soaring above the cliffs in February 1950. (Courtesy of the Soaring Society of America.)

At the Pacific Coast Midwinter Soaring Championships in 1950, the gliderport was rededicated with a special ceremony. Poor weather in February postponed the meet and dedication to March. Later that same year, Gibbs Field in San Diego was renamed and dedicated as Montgomery Field in honor of pioneer aviator John J. Montgomery. (Courtesy of the Gary Fogel Collection.)

William S. "Bill" Ivans was employed at Consolidated Vultee (Convair) in San Diego. His first soaring flight came in 1948 at Torrey Pines in the Associated Glider Clubs of Southern California Schweizer TG-2. He was an avid soaring competitor, member of the Associated Glider Clubs of Southern California, and became president of the Soaring Society of America. (Courtesy of the Soaring Society of America.)

In this photograph, Ivans prepares his new Schweizer 1-23 sailplane during the 1950 Torrey Pines meet. The 1-23 was an all-metal sailplane with superior performance to many of the World War II–era sailplanes. Ivans established a world record for absolute altitude gained in a sailplane of 42,000 feet over the Sierra Nevada in this aircraft. (Courtesy of the Gary Fogel Collection.)

In his sleek Schweizer 1-23, Ivans soars silently by the spectators lining the cliff in 1950. (Courtesy of the Soaring Society of America.)

A Schweizer 1-19 soars by during the fifth annual Pacific Coast Midwinter Soaring Championships in 1951. At one point during the 1951 meet, a total of 17 sailplanes were in the air at the same time soaring up and down the coast. A special public address system was used to keep the spectators informed of the action, with Jim Spurgeon commentating. (Courtesy of the Soaring Society of America.)

Larry Bell was one of the first to "flat top" his World War II–era Laister-Kauffman LK-10 (TG-4A), making the sailplane more aerodynamic. Among other modifications, the fuselage was elongated by two feet, and a bubble canopy was added offering the pilot a 360-degree view. (Courtesy of the Gary Fogel Collection.)

A unique feature of coastal gliderports like Torrey Pines was the ability to soar over the waves of the Pacific and enjoy the laminar winds that come in off the ocean. However, by the 1950s, most of the coastal gliderports of the 1930s had disappeared due to housing development. On windy days at Torrey, good pilots could swoop down to the wave tops and convert their speed back into altitude, climbing all the way back up to ridge top level. Here, Larry Bell makes a flyby in his LK-10. (Courtesy of the Soaring Society of America.)

Postwar San Diego continued to be a focal point for aerospace companies. Many companies also boasted their own internal glider club, with club members soaring on the weekend at Torrey Pines, much in the same way that other employees would take their sailboats out on San Diego Bay. To San Diegans, the gliderport was a wonderful outdoor training ground for ever more efficient aircraft designs. It also became a tourist destination to show the beauty and adventure of silent flight in such a dramatic and scenic location. (Courtesy of the Soaring Society of America.)

Several gliders soar together above the cliffs, using the ridge lift to gain altitude. Pictured on the left is a restored Robin sailplane, then owned by Bob Fronius, who had added a V-tail configuration to the famous sailplane. (Courtesy of Gary Fogel Collection.)

7th ANNUAL

Pacific Coast Mid-Winter Soaring Championships

SATURDAY, FEBRUARY 28, and
SUNDAY, MARCH 1, 1953

Torrey Pines Gliderport

San Diego, California

At each Torrey Pines glider meet, souvenir programs were offered for sale to educate the public about the contestants, events, and the sport of soaring, and to offset the costs involved with event management. (Courtesy of the Gary Fogel Collection.)

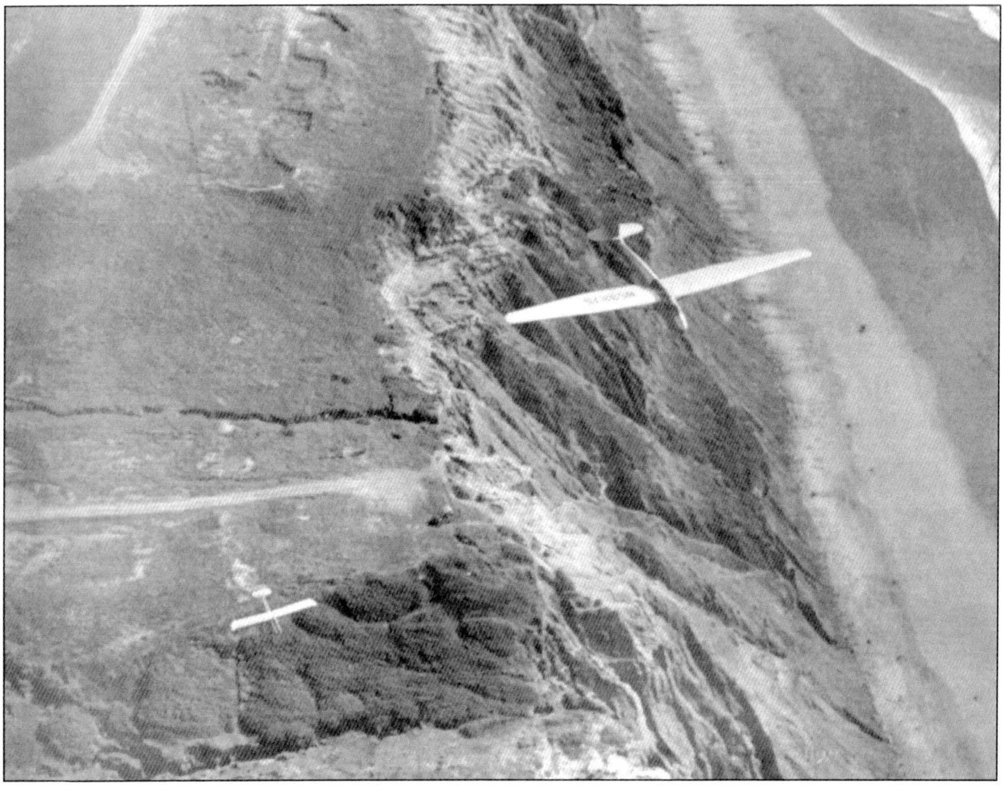

Two Schweizer sailplanes soar over the Torrey Pines cliffs in this aerial view, with empty Black's Beach below. Remnant Camp Callan artillery emplacements can be seen at upper left, the largest mound used by radio-controlled model glider enthusiasts since the mid-1950s. The road between the two gliders ending in a turnaround at the cliff top was used by Torrey pioneers for auto-tow in the 1930s. (Courtesy of the Soaring Society of America.)

Watching the launch of a sailplane from the winch was a bit like watching a kite being reeled up into the sky. Here a Schweizer 2-22 goes up via the winch. Various trucks were used to haul the winch from location to location for club use. Eventually, the winch itself was converted into a trailer that could be towed more easily behind a car or truck. (Courtesy of the George Uvegas Collection.)

Paul Bikle is shown in the cockpit of a Schweizer 1-23 preparing for takeoff at Torrey. Bikle was the director of NASA's Dryden Flight Research Facility at Edwards Air Force Base from 1959 to 1971, in charge of major projects such as the X-15 program. He was also later president of the Soaring Society of America, and set two world records for soaring on February 25, 1961, for absolute altitude (46,267 feet) and absolute altitude gained (42,300 feet). Bikle enjoyed soaring at Torrey Pines, especially during the annual glider meets. (Courtesy of the Bertha Ryan Collection.)

Paul Bikle's Schweizer 1-23 is being hooked up to the winch line at the east end of the gliderport in 1955. (Courtesy of the Gary Fogel Collection.)

Bikle is standing proudly with his "hardware" after winning the 1955 Torrey Pines meet. Bikle not only won the championship for the second time in a row, but he placed first in the altitude, distance, aerobatics, and spot landing categories. His distance flight from Torrey Pines to Oceanside along the coastline for 21.5 miles was the best distance of the meet. (Courtesy of the Soaring Society of America.)

Don Stevens modified his Bowlus Baby Albatross to create what he called a Bowlus "Super Baby Albatross" including wing tip plates and a very pointed nose among other changes. In this photograph, Charles Webber of Pomona holds a balloon at the end of a bamboo pole while Stevens attempted to pop the balloon for the media at the 1956 Torrey Pines meet. Glider meets were typically held over a weekend in February, when the rest of America was far colder. One of Germany's earliest glider pilots from the 1920s, Wolfgang Klemperer, visited the site in 1956 along with his family, as did Col. Floyd Sweet, director of the Soaring Society of America. Klemperer was a cofounder of the Soaring Society of America, and held the first soaring certificate in the world. (Courtesy of the Soaring Society of America.)

Don Mitchell had a lengthy career in soaring, helping Hawley Bowlus with the construction of the prototype Bowlus Baby Albatross in 1937 in San Fernando, as well as building the wings for Essery's *Baby Bomber*, the Bowlus Super Albatross, and other designs. He soon began to design his own Nimbus series of sailplanes. In this photograph, the *Nimbus III* soars at a Torrey Pines meet, capturing the trophy for best new design. (Courtesy of the Gary Fogel Collection.)

Paul and Judy MacCready watch the action from the cliff edge along with other spectators during the 1958 Torrey Pines glider meet. MacCready later credited his time soaring at Torrey Pines with the origin of his philosophy of "doing more with less." This mantra typified soaring, and also the application of drag reduction techniques by MacCready to many other aspects of engineering. Along with Peter Lissaman and a team of engineers, MacCready later developed the *Gossamer Condor*, the first human-powered aircraft to win the Kremer Prize; the *Gossamer Albatross*, the first human-powered aircraft to cross the English Channel; and the *Solar Challenger*, the first solar-powered aircraft to cross the English Channel. (Courtesy of the Soaring Society of America.)

Jack Lambie was a unique fixture of soaring in Southern California, flying his Schweizer 1-26 and Fauvel flying wing. He also pioneered aerodynamic streamlining of his van, which led to collaboration with MacCready on drag reduction methods for trucks. Lambie became a member of MacCready's team that captured the Kremer Prize for the *Gossamer Albatross*. He was also very instrumental in the renaissance of hang gliding in southern California during the 1960s and 1970s, a movement that brought gliding to a new generation of pilots, and brought hang gliding to Torrey Pines. (Courtesy of the George Uvegas Collection.)

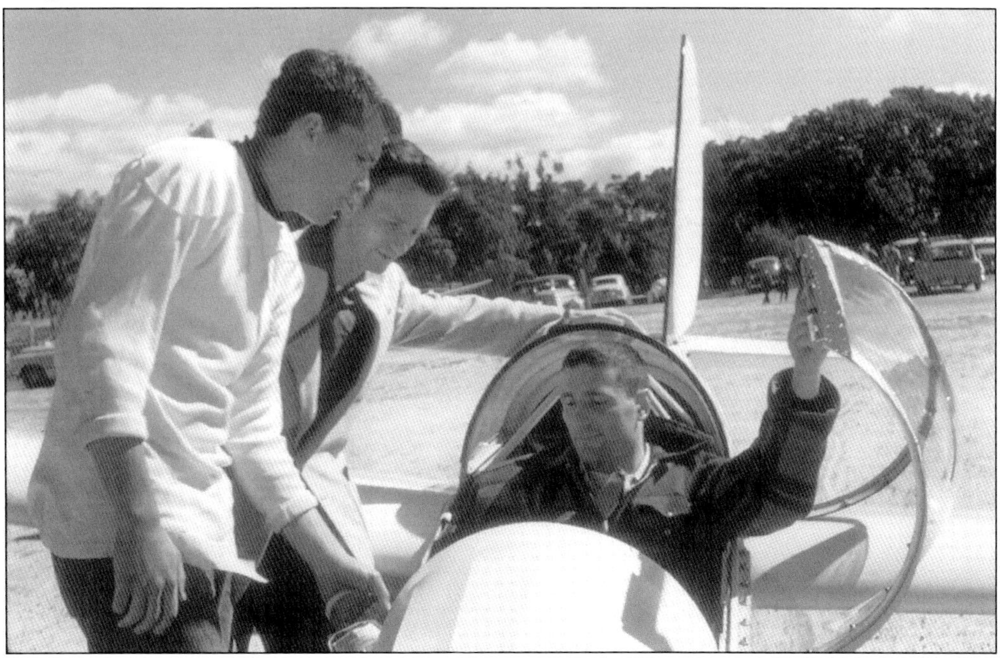

Bruce Carmichael (center) helps assist Jack Lambie (cockpit) in rigging a sack of sand for the "bomb drop" component of the 1956 Torrey Pines meet. Carmichael became an international expert on drag reduction and aerodynamics, and later served twice as president of the Sailplane Homebuilders Association. As a part of the bomb drop, competitors released their sack of sand after winch release and attempted to hit a chalked bull's eye on the ground below. (Courtesy of the Bertha Ryan Collection.)

Irving Prue's Prue 215 was an unusual V-tail homebuilt sailplane. Working as an engineer for Lockheed Aircraft Company, Prue was highly skilled in sailplane design and construction. Harold Hutchinson flew a Prue 215 to second place at the 1958 United States Soaring Nationals. (Courtesy of the Bertha Ryan Collection.)

From left to right, Ray Parker, Shirley Hall, and Bill Royce chat before Parker launches in the Parker PJ-1 *Tiny Mite* in 1956. Another "midget" sailplane, the *Tiny Mite* was built by Ray Parker and Richard Johnson and made use of a special wheeled dolly for takeoff (visible below the aircraft). The dolly dropped once the sailplane became airborne. (Courtesy of the Bertha Ryan Collection.)

Associated Glider Clubs of Southern California instructor John Swinson congratulates newest club member Keith "Tweedie" Allen with a traditional dousing of water after his first solo flight at Torrey Pines, made precisely to the minute of his 14th birthday. Many young pilots learned to fly at Torrey Pines in the venerable club Schweizer TG-2 as federal regulations allowed students to fly solo as early as age 14. Another member of the club, Bob Storck, also soloed on his 14th birthday one year later at Torrey Pines. (Courtesy of the Gary Fogel Collection.)

Ernie Shattuck and John Swinson enjoyed many hours of soaring above the cliffs at Torrey Pines in their co-owned Schweizer TG-2. (Courtesy of the Gary Fogel Collection.)

When the tide was high, pilots had to be careful to be sure the lift would be sufficient to land on top of the cliffs again, or they risked an unplanned water adventure. (Courtesy of the Gary Fogel Collection.)

Upwind landings such as this one toward the west over the eucalyptus trees were made in high-wind conditions. The foundation from the former Camp Callan postal exchange warehouse is visible in the foreground. This foundation continues to be used as a tie-down area for sailplanes during their annual operation at the gliderport. (Courtesy of the Gary Fogel Collection.)

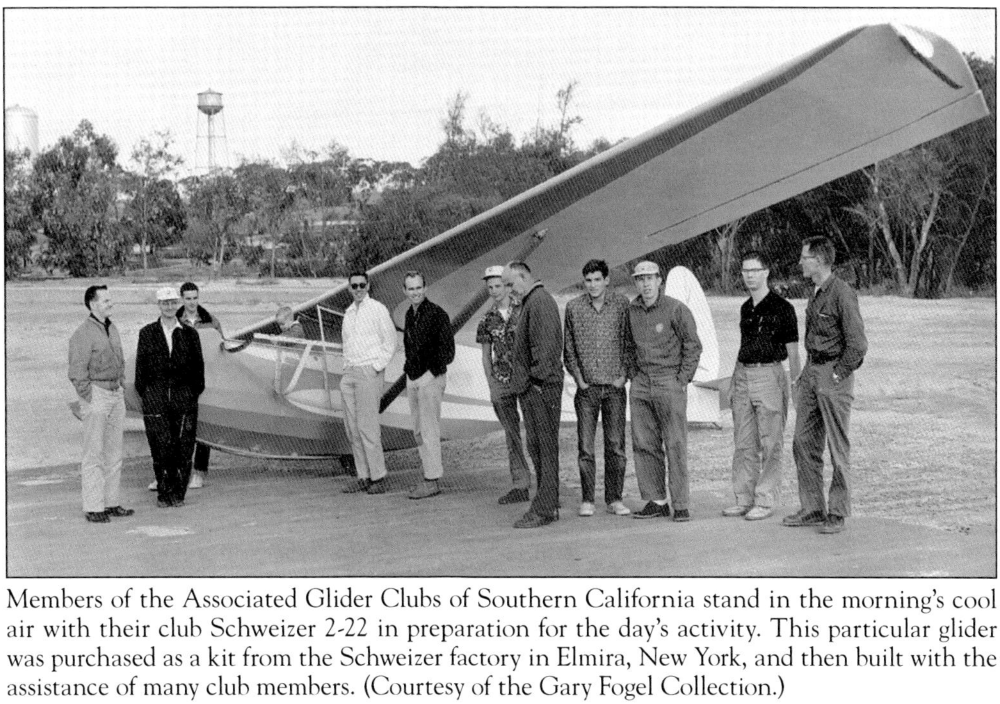

Members of the Associated Glider Clubs of Southern California stand in the morning's cool air with their club Schweizer 2-22 in preparation for the day's activity. This particular glider was purchased as a kit from the Schweizer factory in Elmira, New York, and then built with the assistance of many club members. (Courtesy of the Gary Fogel Collection.)

The Schweizer 2-22 was a solid training glider, pictured here just prior to winch launch. (Courtesy of the Gary Fogel Collection.)

The Associated Glider Clubs of Southern California also purchased its own Piper Cubs to tow the gliders at the gliderport. The Cubs were used to pull the sailplanes with a rope to altitude, with the sailplanes releasing and continuing their soaring adventure while the towplane returned to the gliderport for the next tow. This process was called aerotowing. Towplanes used either the main runway or the cross-diagonal runway for aerotowing operations. (Courtesy of the Gary Fogel Collection.)

An aerotow operation with a Piper Cub pulling a sailplane aloft from the main gliderport runway towards the west is pictured here. The 90-horsepower engine on the Cub could be coaxed into the task of pulling a two-place sailplane aloft, so long as there was sufficient runway. (Courtesy of the Soaring Society of America.)

Two Piper Cubs are at work, one pulling up a sailplane along the diagonal runway towards the northwest, the other preparing to return for a landing to pull up the next sailplane. Operations such as these required significant radio coordination between pilots, and crowd control was necessary for the many spectators who would turn out simply to watch the activities. This particular photograph was taken during one of the many Pacific Coast Midwinter Soaring Championships, as evidenced by the hundreds of cars parked to the southeast. (Courtesy of the Gary Fogel Collection.)

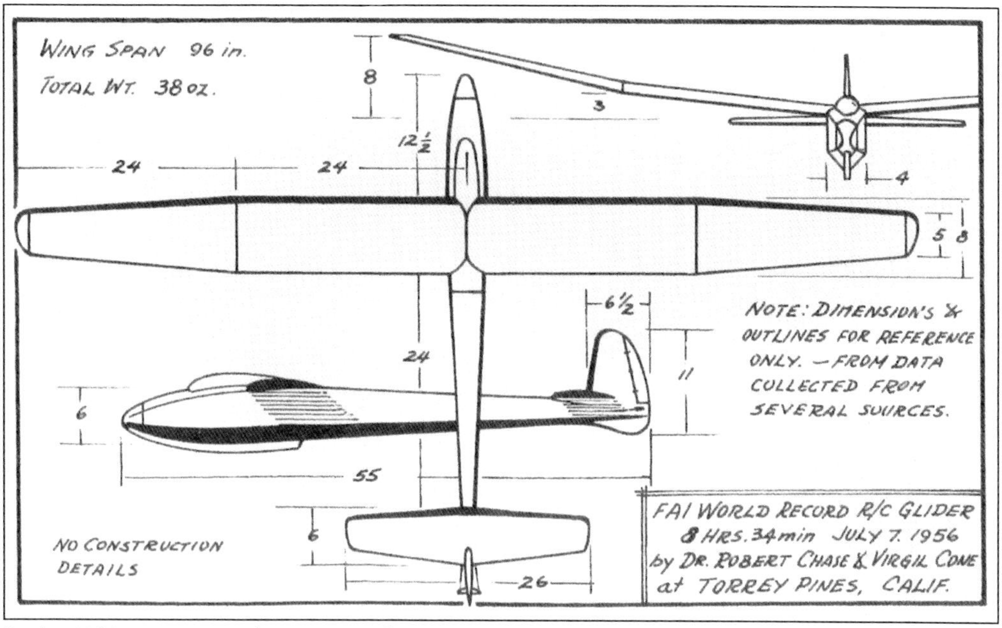

In the 1950s, amateur radio operators began to experiment with radio-controlled model sailplanes. Dr. Bob Chase flew this early design in 1956 to a world record of 8 hours and 34 minutes at Torrey Pines using only rudder control. (Courtesy of the Gary Fogel Collection.)

A Schweizer 1-19 makes a close pass by the cliff edge for the spectators. (Courtesy of the Gary Fogel Collection.)

During large glider meetings, pilot briefings were held every morning to review rules and safety procedures. Here the many pilots and their teams shiver prior to the first launch of the day. Two water towers from Camp Callan visible in the background remained for many years after the closure of the Army base. (Courtesy of the Gary Fogel Collection.)

From left to right, Bob Snelker, Frank Kernes, and Ray Parker pose for the cameras with the *Tiny Mite* as David McKay's flat-topped Schweizer 1-26 sits to the right. Other sailplanes are being assembled in the background as contestants prepare for the meet. (Courtesy of the Gary Fogel Collection.)

Art Daegling (far right) prepares his beautiful Bowlus Baby Albatross for a soaring flight. Bob Storck (center, with coffee) assisted Daegling as a crew member, having learned to soar under the instruction of Sterling Starr and Bill Ivans. In 1959, Storck successfully launched in a Bowlus Baby Albatross at Torrey Pines using a horse to tow the sailplane aloft. (Courtesy of the Gary Fogel Collection.)

The graceful and classic lines of the Bowlus Baby Albatross became an American soaring icon. In this photograph, Art Daegling's Baby Albatross awaits winch launch. (Courtesy of the Gary Fogel Collection.)

Another Bowlus Baby Albatross arrives on final approach for a downwind landing at the gliderport. After the war, the large graded obstacle course area from Camp Callan was converted into a long paved runway for takeoff, and just to its north, a long dirt runway for landing. By 1956, this landing approach skirted a fence separating the gliderport from the newly completed Torrey Pines Municipal Golf Course, forcing the gliderport to shift its landing runway slightly to the south. (Courtesy of the San Diego Air and Space Museum.)

Ted Grabosky in his flat-topped Laister-Kauffman LK-10 makes his best effort to stop before hitting the plastic cone marking the spot landing competition. This particular LK-10 was modified by Jack Green, Ernie Shattuck, and John Williams and flown by Helen Dick. The sandy surface of the graded runway combined with the loose pebbles naturally found in the soil made spot landings very challenging. (Courtesy of the Gary Fogel Collection.)

In the 1950s, spectators parked their cars on the southern portion of the gliderport. Thousands of spectators watched the action from the point of takeoff and also from along the cliff edge. In this photograph, spectators observe a sailplane making a spot landing. (Courtesy of the Gary Fogel Collection.)

Art Daegling stops his Bowlus Baby Albatross just in time while crowds of spectators watch from the hillside to the south. (Courtesy of the Gary Fogel Collection.)

Lloyd Licher prepares for a flight in a Schweizer 1-7 in February 1958. Lloyd was executive secretary for the Soaring Society of America, became executive director, and was also editor of *Soaring* magazine. Later in the 1970s, Licher was instrumental in the formation of the Southern California Hang Gliding Association and edited its journal *Ground Skimmer*. (Courtesy of the Bertha Ryan Collection.)

At the 1959 Torrey Pines meet, the president of the Soaring Society of America, Harner Selvidge (front), flew his Schweizer 2-22C along with Ted Sharp (rear), who served as treasurer of the Soaring Society of America. (Courtesy of the Soaring Society of America.)

Many local glider pilots designed, built, and flew their own homebuilt sailplanes. Wade Steinruck was no exception, shown here launching in his Steinruck V-tail sailplane called the *SCS-1*. The *SCS-1* was designed by A. Cordas and built and completed by Steinruck in 1959. Gene Whigham, George Tweed, Ken Coward, and others also built their own sailplanes and flew them at Torrey Pines. (Courtesy of the San Diego Air and Space Museum.)

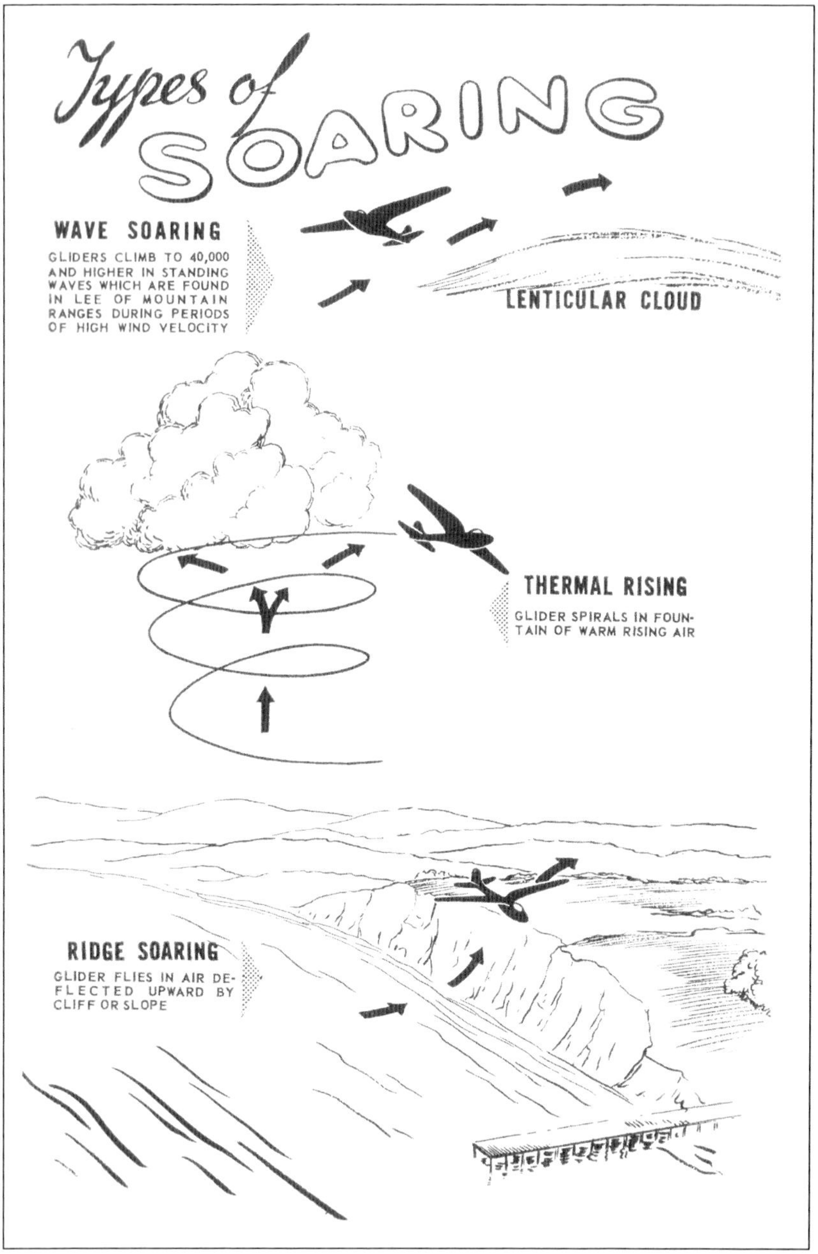

The Torrey Pines Gliderport was popular for ridge soaring, where sea breezes deflected upwards created lift. Thermal currents under clouds were also used, and provided the opportunity for greater altitude and distance. During the 1950s, however, an entirely new type of soaring was discovered, making use of high-altitude stationary waves in the atmosphere. High-altitude waves above the Sierra Nevada Mountains were researched by a team of expert glider pilots including John Robinson, Paul MacCready, Ray Parker, Harland Ross, and others. They succeeded in generating an improved understanding of the atmospheric conditions that generate the wave, leading to clear-air turbulence avoidance for passenger aircraft. Glider pilots also quickly recognized that these same conditions could be used to establish tremendously high world records for altitude. (Courtesy of the Gary Fogel Collection).

Six

THE 1960S

An aerial view of the Torrey Pines cliffs shows the paved gliderport main runway and the diagonal, as well as construction for the new Torrey Pines Municipal Golf Course to the north and La Jolla Farms to the south. The many empty fields to the east of the gliderport provided ample opportunity for cross-country soaring given the many possible off-field landing zones. (Courtesy of the San Diego Air and Space Museum.)

John Swinson looks pleasantly surprised to have found Valerie Benson on his wing. Benson was meet queen for the 1960 Pacific Coast Midwinter Soaring Championships. Many of the glider meets also included a queen selected by the San Diego Junior Chamber of Commerce. At the 1957 meet, local La Jolla High School junior Jo Raquel Tejada was chosen as the meet queen. She later gained fame as movie actress Raquel Welch. (Courtesy of the Gary Fogel Collection.)

A Schweizer 1-26 hugs the coastline in search of ridge lift over some spectators. The 1-26 was a mid-wing sailplane produced by the Schweizer Aircraft Corporation first introduced in the 1950s, gaining wide popularity across America in the 1960s. (Courtesy of the Soaring Society of America.)

Torrey Pines was a perfect match for the 1-26. In this photograph, the Antelope Valley Soaring Club's Schweizer 1-26 makes a run to the north during the 1960 Torrey Pines Meet. (Courtesy of the Soaring Society of America.)

Another Schweizer 1-26 makes a speed run to the north, tracking the ridgeline in search of every small bump of lift possible. (Courtesy of the Bertha Ryan Collection.)

The French Fauvel AV-36 flying wing sailplane was flown by Jack Lambie at Torrey Pines. Very unusual for its time, this was the only Fauvel AV-36 operating in the United States. (Courtesy of the Soaring Society of America.)

The 1960 Pacific Coast Midwinter Soaring Championship winners pictured here are, from left to right, Larry Bell holding the helmet he won for second place (he also took the duration contest with a flight of just over four hours), Ted Grabowsky (dual distance winner), Dave McNay (meet champion), meet queen Valerie Benson holding the Montgomery Trophy, Lloyd Licher (winner of the bomb drop contest), one of the Linn brothers representing the Soarcerers Club (winners of the club participation trophy), and Stan Winsor (winner of the spot landing contest, with a distance of one and five-eighths inches from the mark). (Courtesy of the Gary Fogel Collection.)

Into his third decade of soaring at Torrey Pines, Ray Parker enjoys a flight in Lynn Christensen's Laister-Kauffman LK-10 during the 1962 Torrey Pines meet. (Courtesy of the Soaring Society of America.)

Bruce Beebe, an architect from San Francisco, enjoyed participating in the Torrey Pines meets. Here, he prepares for takeoff via winch tow next to his sleek Schleicher Ka-6CR sailplane. (Courtesy of the George Uvegas Collection.)

Beebe had an exceptional flight in the Ka-6CR during the 1963 meet, managing to soar all the way to Brawley, California, near the Salton Sea, a distance of 100 miles, from winch launch. During the same meet, Ray Proenneke flew his Cherokee II from an aerotow launch to Desert Center, a distance of 116 miles. However, Beebe was declared meet champion because of the higher points placed on distance flights via winch launch versus those that started from airplane launch. (Courtesy of the Soaring Society of America.)

Sterling Starr is pictured in his Schweizer 1-23D. Starr was another exceptional pilot from the San Diego area who completed the 11th Diamond C badge in the United States and later served as president of the Soaring Society of America. Starr learned to soar with the Associated Glider Clubs of Southern California in 1953, first at Lake Elsinore, and then with a TG-2 at Torrey Pines, becoming a certified instructor in 1957. That same year, he made a flight of 333 miles in his 1-23 from Bishop, California, to Escalante, Utah, to capture the Soaring Society of America's Barringer Trophy for the longest flight of any American sailplane pilot for that year. (Courtesy of the George Uvegas Collection.)

Winners of the 18th Pacific Coast Midwinter Soaring Championships in 1964 are, from left to right, Sterling Starr (second place), Lenore Plummer (meet queen), Ray Proenneke (meet champion), and Larry Bell (third place). Competitors came from all over the west, including California, Arizona, New Mexico, Washington, and even one contestant—Ted Sanford—from Washington, DC. Sanford had previously been score keeper for many years for the Torrey meets. Pilots who made distance flights from Torrey during the meet were required to return back via car before the end of the meet. On the last day of the meet, Starr made a flight of 41 miles to a landing near Cuyamaca Peak, and Proenneke made a flight of 31 miles to Ramona. Both pilots made it back just before the meet ended at 4:00 p.m. to officially register their scores. (Courtesy of the Soaring Society of America.)

Sterling Starr soars in his Schweizer 1-23HM along the cliffs at Torrey Pines. (Courtesy of the Sterling Starr Collection.)

Serving as a member of the Woman Airforce Service Pilots (known as WASPs) during World War II, Helen Dick took an interest in serving as a towing pilot for the Associated Glider Clubs of Southern California. She quickly discovered the joy of soaring at Torrey Pines and later helped to pioneer soaring routes through the northern Owens Valley. She became the first American woman to achieve the Diamond C badge, and was the first woman elected director of the Soaring Society of America. She is pictured here in her Zugvogel III at Torrey Pines. (Courtesy of the Bertha Ryan Collection.)

Walt Mooney was a central component of many types of aviation in Southern California during the 1960s. He was known internationally for his many model airplane plans published in *Model Airplane News*, *Boy's Life*, *AeroModeler*, and *Model Builder* magazines. He helped popularize the now-famous "peanut scale" rubber band–powered model airplanes, perhaps designing more of them than anyone else in the world. An avid glider pilot, Mooney was also a member of the Associated Glider Clubs of Southern California, enjoying many hours with the club at Torrey Pines and other locations. He was the master of ceremonies for the 20th annual Torrey Pines meet in 1966. (Courtesy of the Soaring Society of America.)

Fred Daams's homebuilt *Falcon* sailplane was a chimera, with wings from a Laister-Kauffman LK-10, fuselage from a drop tank, a canopy from an F-84 fighter jet, and vertical tail and elevators from a Cessna 140. (Courtesy of the George Uvegas Collection.)

Daams's *Falcon* is soaring over the Pacific at Torrey Pines as photographed by acclaimed soaring photographer George Uvegas. (Courtesy of the George Uvegas Collection.)

The Associated Glider Clubs of Southern California boasted a membership of over 100 pilots, with a monthly newsletter titled *Wind and Wings*. Club members soared on the weekends at Torrey Pines, Lake Elsinore, Warner Springs, and Jacumba. (Courtesy of the Gary Fogel Collection.)

Many children were kept busy filling paper bags with sand in preparation for the friendly bomb drop component of the 1966 Torrey Pines meet. (Courtesy of the Soaring Society of America.)

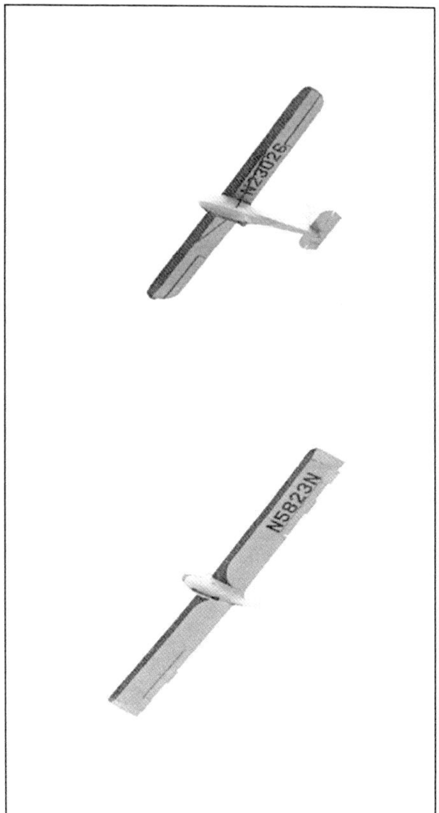

Jim Marske's *XM-1D* flying wing soars under a Schweizer 1-7 at Torrey Pines. The Marske flying wing was a very modern design in 1960 relative to the older 1939-vintage Schweizer 1-7. The Schweizer 1-7 pictured here is now part of the collection of the National Soaring Museum in Elmira, New York. (Courtesy of the George Uvegas Collection.)

Pictured here is a room full of Torrey Pines meet champions, including some of the greats of American soaring. From left to right are Herman Stiglmeier, John Williams, John Loufek, Dave McNay, Pete Peterson, Paul Bikle, Jack Lambie, Dave Boone, Paul MacCready, Sterling Starr, and Larry Bell. In front of them is a large cake in celebration of the 20th anniversary of the Pacific Coast Midwinter Soaring Championships. (Courtesy of the Soaring Society of America.)

Judy Vaughn was the queen of the 1967 Pacific Coast Midwinter Soaring Championships. The meet was so popular with the press that the Goodyear blimp was overhead so that television crews could have better shots. Some of the meets during the 1960s were broadcast on NBC's *Wide Wide World*. (Courtesy of the George Uvegas Collection.)

An aerial view of the gliderport from 1967 shows the bomb drop target (1), the diagonal runway used for aerial towing (2), the winch location (3), the landing runway (4), the sailplane tie-down area (5), the winch launch area (6), the spectator area (7), the primary runway for winch operations (8), and the aerotow launch area (9). The neighboring Salk Institute at center right opened in 1963. The institute bordered the gliderport on its southern edge, on the same hillside where spectators of the 1950s glider meets parked their cars. To the east, Interstate 5 was under construction, and Genesee Avenue and North Torrey Pines Road are clearly visible, along with outlines of former Camp Callan facilities. (Courtesy of the Soaring Society of America.)

Another aerial view of the gliderport in the late 1960s, looking toward the southwest, shows the golf course to the north of the gliderport, the Salk Institute to the south, Torrey Pines Road to the east, and the Pacific Ocean to the west. Once very remote to San Diego, by the early 1960s the gliderport was under considerable pressure. Half of the gliderport property was deeded to the regents of the University of California by the citizens of San Diego for the purpose of establishing a campus at La Jolla. Chancellor Roger Revelle expressed a desire for gliding to continue as an educational asset to the young campus. As a result, the University of California San Diego Glider Club was born, with members of the Associated Glider Clubs of Southern California assisting students with glider training. (Courtesy of the San Diego Air and Space Museum.)

During the glider meets of the late 1960s, a control tower was established near the junction of the main runway and the diagonal runway to coordinate the many winch launches, aerotowing operations, and landings. (Courtesy of the George Uvegas Collection.)

From the control tower it was possible to truly watch all of the soaring activities. Here, a gaggle of pilots enjoys a passing thermal in an attempt to gain points for duration and altitude. Bold pilots would set off for cross-country flights from these thermals, with chase teams following them by car in radio communication. (Courtesy of the George Uvegas Collection.)

Harry Baldwin was a regular participant at the annual Pacific Coast Midwinter event, but he was also a strong supporter of the Associated Glider Clubs of Southern California as well as the 1-26 Association, a national organization of pilots who enjoy flying the Schweizer 1-26. Harry and his purple and white 1-26 flew to many national 1-26 championships. (Courtesy of the George Uvegas Collection.)

Baldwin and his Schweizer 1-26 are soaring effortlessly on the ridge lift. On one flight in his 1-26, Baldwin soared from a winch launch all the way to Desert Center, California, the longest flight of any sailplane from Torrey Pines following winch launch. (Courtesy of the George Uvegas Collection.)

Harry Baldwin is on a downwind final approach for landing at Torrey Pines directly over the same road that was used by 1930s pilots for auto-tows. (Courtesy of the George Uvegas Collection.)

After a spot landing, officials used a plumb bob from the nose to mark the stopping point, measuring the distance in inches from the actual target spot with a ruler. Expert pilots would be able to stop their planes within just a few inches of the mark. The club winch is visible on the hill to the upper left. (Courtesy of the George Uvegas Collection.)

Sylvia Colton gives the tail of a Schweizer 1-26 a hug for good behavior. Colton was president of the Associated Glider Clubs of Southern California during the late 1960s. She and her husband, Joe Colton, helped maintain club enthusiasm and kept the gliderport operational. (Courtesy of the George Uvegas Collection.)

At the 1968 Torrey Pines Meet, a rare 1935-vintage Göppingen Gö3 Minimoa owned by George Kern graced the skies of Torrey Pines with its gull wings. The German Minimoa is one of the most recognized sailplanes in history, shown here on the cover of the 1969 Torrey Pines meet program. (Courtesy of the Gary Fogel Collection.)

This is a bird's-eye view taken while soaring north along the cliffs, following a Schweizer 1-26. The Piper Cub on the beach awaits any sailplanes forced to land there due to a lull in the wind, towing them aerially back to the top of the cliffs. (Courtesy of the Soaring Society of America.)

The John J. Montgomery Memorial Championship Trophy of the Pacific Coast Midwinter Soaring Championships is pictured here. The perpetual trophy was coveted by glider pilots and became the symbol of the longest running annual contest at any one location in American soaring history. (Courtesy of the George Uvegas Collection.)

Seven

"Kitty Hawk of the West"

In the late 1960s and early 1970s, radio-control enthusiasts used the Torrey Pines Gliderport with increasing regularity. One of these enthusiasts, Mark Smith, developed radio-controlled flying gulls that were used in the movie *Jonathan Livingston Seagull*. The movie was filmed in part at the gliderport. Smith also became a champion model sailplane pilot and produced the Wanderer model sailplane, which was sold in mass quantities worldwide. (Courtesy of the Gary Fogel Collection.)

A new breed of exceptional sailplane designers and pilots was born, using the gliderport to help refine their model sailplane efficiency. In this photograph, Harris Nelson launches one of his many designs. As with the manned counterparts, many local modelers have competed at the highest levels in both national and international competition. (Courtesy of the Gary Fogel Collection.)

Model soaring held its own aesthetic beauty, as Dr. Scott Jenkins demonstrates with his highly modified straight-wing Hobie Hawk sailplane at sunset. (Courtesy of the Gary Fogel Collection.)

As radio technology improved, the models became more precise in their ability to mimic all of the functions of manned sailplanes. Dr. Larry Fogel helped usher in these larger fiberglass sailplanes at Torrey Pines. (Courtesy of the Gary Fogel Collection.)

During the early 1970s, hang glider enthusiasts also came to Torrey Pines, recognizing the superior soaring conditions that exist at the location. Four world records for hang glider endurance were established between 1972 and 1973—Taras Kiceniuk Jr. (1 hour, 11 minutes; 2 hours, 26 minutes), Bob Wills (3 hours, 3 minutes), and Mike Mitchell (3 hours, 45 minutes). The *Icarus II* flying wing glider developed by Kiceniuk was the first controllable soaring hang glider. Kiceniuk later assisted Paul MacCready with the *Gossamer Condor*. (Courtesy of the Gary Fogel Collection.)

An early Rogallo-style hang glider launches from the cliff edge. (Courtesy of the Gary Fogel Collection.)

Award-winning hang glider photographer Bettina Gray captures Bill Liscomb launching in a Quicksilver, while Rich Findley and Ron Johnson assist as wire men. (Courtesy of the Gary Fogel Collection.)

By the late 1980s, paragliders also came on the scene at Torrey Pines, with their colorful airfoil-equipped parachutes allowing them to float over the cliffs. (Courtesy of the Gary Fogel Collection.)

Over time, their design and construction also improved, and just like the manned sailplanes, model sailplanes, and hang gliders before them, paraglider pilots have learned to enjoy the cliffs for their invisible lift. (Courtesy of the Gary Fogel Collection.)

In the early 1990s, a series of historical designations were placed on the Torrey Pines Gliderport, first as a National Soaring Landmark of the National Soaring Museum in Elmira, New York, then as a San Diego City Historic Site (No. 315), then on the California Register of Historic Places, and finally on the National Register of Historic Places—the first gliderport in the nation to receive such an honor. Later, the gliderport was also dedicated as the first National Model Aviation Heritage Site in the nation by the Academy of Model Aeronautics. Here, Dr. Larry Fogel addresses the crowd for the 1993 dedication of the site as a City Historic Site. (Courtesy of the Gary Fogel Collection.)

The dedication ceremonies included special visitors such as Woody Brown, who was not only recognized as a pioneer at Torrey Pines, but was honored with a special luau by the surfers at Windansea. (Courtesy of the Gary Fogel Collection.)

Paul MacCready epitomized the importance of locations like the Torrey Pines Gliderport. MacCready continued his accomplishments in engineering, converting his knowledge of aerodynamics and silent flight to the design of the General Motors EV-1 electric car, and unmanned aerial vehicles capable of flight over 80,000 feet in the atmosphere as a part of his company, AeroVironment. MacCready credited his victory at the 1947 Torrey Pines meet as a catalyst for other technical achievements. He sought to help preserve the gliderport as a marriage of technology and nature. (Courtesy of the Gary Fogel Collection.)

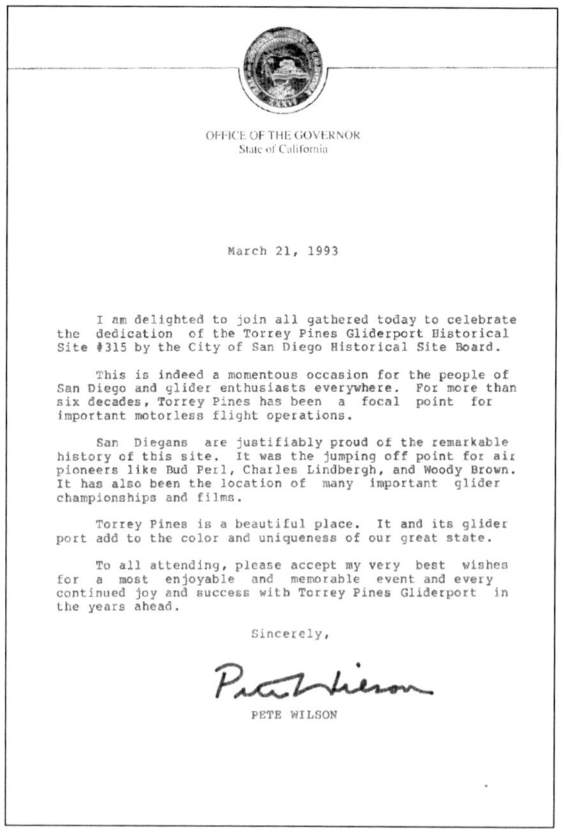

OFFICE OF THE GOVERNOR
State of California

March 21, 1993

I am delighted to join all gathered today to celebrate the dedication of the Torrey Pines Gliderport Historical Site #315 by the City of San Diego Historical Site Board.

This is indeed a momentous occasion for the people of San Diego and glider enthusiasts everywhere. For more than six decades, Torrey Pines has been a focal point for important motorless flight operations.

San Diegans are justifiably proud of the remarkable history of this site. It was the jumping off point for air pioneers like Bud Perl, Charles Lindbergh, and Woody Brown. It has also been the location of many important glider championships and films.

Torrey Pines is a beautiful place. It and its glider port add to the color and uniqueness of our great state.

To all attending, please accept my very best wishes for a most enjoyable and memorable event and every continued joy and success with Torrey Pines Gliderport in the years ahead.

Sincerely,

Pete Wilson

PETE WILSON

Letters of support for the preservation of the Torrey Pines Gliderport as a unique recreational resource for California came from all over, including the governor at the time, Pete Wilson. (Courtesy of the Gary Fogel Collection.)

THE WHITE HOUSE

WASHINGTON

May 14, 1993

I am delighted that the Torrey Pines Gliderport has been designated a historic site by the City of San Diego.

Torrey Pines is part of a rich aviation tradition in Southern California. Since Professor John Montgomery's pioneer flight in 1884, thousands of Americans have enjoyed Torrey Pines' famous bluffs and stunning ocean views. Torrey Pines has played an important role in the development of new technology -- from the Robinson variometer to the Dead-man pulley take-off system -- and its natural beauty and serendipitous location have greatly advanced the sport of soaring.

As the only remaining gliderport in America that is directly adjacent to the Pacific Ocean, Torrey Pines serves as an extraordinary site for the enjoyment of all Americans who are interested in the wonders of human flight.

Bill Clinton

Even President Clinton voiced his pleasure that the gliderport was preserved for the future of all those interested in soaring of any kind. (Courtesy of the Gary Fogel Collection.)

The historic Torrey Pines Gliderport captures the beauty of soaring flight in a way that few other locations in the world can. (Courtesy of the George Uvegas Collection.)

Bibliography

Big Blue Sky: The Untold Story of Hang Gliding—The First Extreme Sport. Video written, directed, produced, and narrated by William P. Liscomb, 2008.

Daly-Lipe, Patricia and Barbara Dawson (Steele Lipe, ed.). *La Jolla: A Celebration of Its Past.* San Diego: Sunbelt Publications, 2002.

Fogel, Gary. *Wind and Wings: The History of Soaring in San Diego.* San Diego: Rock Reef Publishing Company, 2000.

Harwood, Craig S. and Gary B. Fogel. *Quest for Flight: John J. Montgomery and the Dawn of Aviation in the West.* Norman, OK: University of Oklahoma Press, 2012.

Lincoln, Joseph Colville. *Soaring on the Wind: A Photographic Essay on Silent Flight.* Flagstaff, AZ: Northland Press, 1972.

Lindbergh, Anne Morrow. *Hour of Gold, Hour of Lead: Diaries and Letters of Anne Morrow Lindbergh, 1929–1932.* New York: Harcourt Brace Jovanovich, 1973.

Of Wind and Waves: The Life of Woody Brown. Produced and Directed by David L. Brown, 2006.

Save Our Heritage Organization: Four Decades of Historic Preservation in San Diego County. Video filmed and directed by Dan Soderberg, 2009.

Schweizer, Paul A. *Wings Like Eagles: The Story of Soaring in the United States.* Washington, DC: Smithsonian Institution Press, 1988.

Short, Simine. *Glider Mail.* Cinnaminson, NJ: The American Air Mail Society, 1987.

Soaring Torrey Pines. Video written, directed, produced, and narrated by William P. Liscomb and La Jolla Historical Society, 2010.

Streetman, Joe W. *The Lindberghs Soar in San Diego.* San Diego: Joe W. Streetman, 2000.

Stieri, Emanuele. *Gliders and Glider Training.* New York: Essential Books, 1943.

Teale, Edwin W. *The Book of Gliders.* New York: E.P. Dutton and Company, 1930.

Winters, Kathleen C. *Anne Morrow Lindbergh: First Lady of the Air.* New York: Palgrave Macmillan, 2006.

.R THOUSANDS OF LOCAL HISTORY BOOKS
.ATURING MILLIONS OF VINTAGE IMAGES

.adia Publishing, the leading local history publisher in the United States, . committed to making history accessible and meaningful through publishing books that celebrate and preserve the heritage of America's people and places.

Find more books like this at
www.arcadiapublishing.com

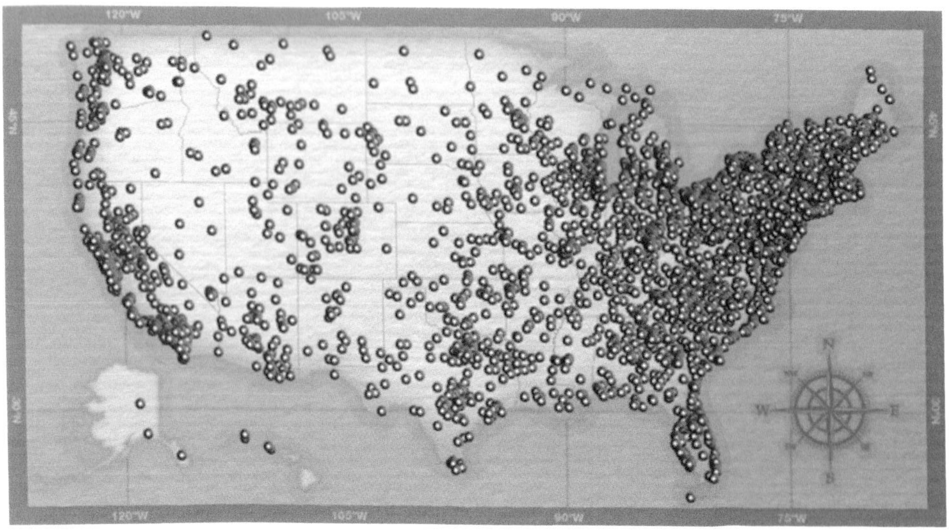

Search for your hometown history, your old stomping grounds, and even your favorite sports team.

Consistent with our mission to preserve history on a local level, this book was printed in South Carolina on American-made paper and manufactured entirely in the United States. Products carrying the accredited Forest Stewardship Council (FSC) label are printed on 100 percent FSC-certified paper.

MADE IN THE USA